Hathor, Master of Sound & Love

Keys to Healing and Self-Mastery according to the Hathors
by Ricardo B Serrano, R.Ac.

"Bright but hidden, the Self dwells in the heart."

A Guide for Emotional and Self-Mastery,
Healing and Stress Management

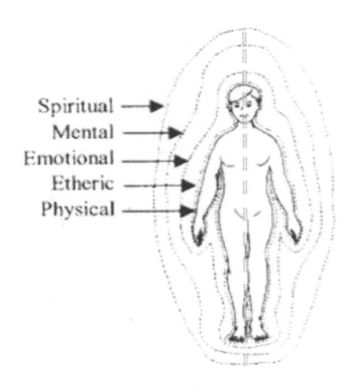

Spiritual →
Mental →
Emotional →
Etheric →
Physical →

Keys to Healing and Self-Mastery
according to the Hathors
by Ricardo B Serrano, R.Ac.

"You must build the *Ka;* you must build the life-force."
— Hathors

A Guide for Emotional and Self-Mastery,

Healing and Stress Management

Keys to Healing and Self-Mastery
according to the Hathors

By Ricardo B Serrano, R.Ac.
ISBN 978-0-9877819-8-7

DISCLAIMER: Ricardo B Serrano will not be held liable for any adverse effects arising from the meditation practices and the recommended Dr. Budwig diet. The physical and psychological conditions of each person vary. If adverse effects are experienced, stop the practice of the meditations and/or diet immediately.

DEDICATIONS

To every practitioner of the Omkabah Heart Lightbody Activation,
Holographic Sound Healing, meditation and Qigong of every tradition
and to my Kashmir Shaivism spiritual gurus.

"The heart is the hub of all sacred places, go there and roam."

Bhagawan Nityananda

I AM SHIVA

"God and the individual are one, to realize this is the essence of Shaivism."

Swami Lakshmanjoo

May the grace of Lord Shiva shine upon you.

TABLE OF CONTENTS

Caution: Do not practice *Ka (Merkaba) Meditation Procedure* without first training to root to Mother Earth to avoid self induced energetic psychosis.

FOREWORD

By Anne Shirley Serrano

When I hear the word "guru" I automatically see my father. To spell the word guru I find myself looking into my father's eyes speaking, "Jee, you are you (G-U-R-U)," a phonetic bell rings in my ear. The enlightened hum begins as he touches the keys on the redwood piano and softly sings to his new born child fast asleep in her cradle. From what I have witnessed in my father is that a guru is a spiritual leader who blesses their pupils with loving oms and teaches far eastern philosophical virtues to ultimately spiritual awaken the One state of being in All That Is. To every daughter her father is invincible; the man whom she runs to when afraid or calls when in need of help. Ricardo B Serrano life's study and service to mankind is to free those from human suffering and spiritually awaken existence into celestial ascension. Ricardo is a living healer, my hero is my father.

Through the millennia Jesus Christ embodies a story of never-ending hope so it is imperative to remember that from his consciousness he has said "The Father and I are one."

Upon opening this book it is the upmost endearing pleasure to greet you as a reader looking into the lettered light of black on white. In between the lines you will find an info realm of burning colors that touch on questions that are then conveyed in answers of insight to your well being. Your feelings are, in fact, an emotion you experience. The sensation in what one particular reacts is the living gratitude one embodies. Beauty cannot be denied as well as how the truth never dies in its entirety. You in the loving flesh as eyes of the beholder are about to witness words of positive guidance. Writings by a scientist, a musician, a doctor, and an artist in whom all have your best interest in mind have been collectively gathered for your knowledge, for your self empowerment. When we are one, generally speaking as writer and reader, we have come to an understanding. To understand is to accept as to receive is to tolerate willingly. True coexistence with one another and especially yourself is the formless love you will be able to practice.

To have a profound understanding of your personal divinity in existence is to be here there and everywhere, in other words, is to have a pantheistic approach. Pantheism is a God concept, a thought form whose sole purpose is to identify the individual with that one state of being. A holy one is only one and you are one of many on this planet in which we live. Home is where our story begins so never forget that Earth is first on your journey to spiritual ascension.

So as you turn these pages and pass the words remember: that where God is is where you are. In this universe of the extraordinaire *You and I verse.*

PREFACE

"Meditate on Om as the Self." – Mundaka Upanishad 2.2.3

"Bright but hidden, the Self dwells in the heart.
Everything that moves, breathes, opens, and closes
Lives in the Self. He is the source of love
And may be known through love but not through thought
He is the goal of life. Attain this goal!"
– Mundaka Upanishad 112, 113

"The Self is hidden in the lotus of the heart.
Those who see themselves in all the creatures go
day by day into the world of Brahman hidden
in the heart. Established in peace, they rise
above body consciousness to the supreme
light of the Self. Immortal, free from fear, this
Self is Brahman, called the True. Beyond the
mortal and the immortal, he binds both worlds
together. Those who know this live day after
day in heaven in this very life."
– Chandogya Upanishad 192-193

"It moves and It moves not. It is far and also It is near.
It is within and also It is without all this.
It is near to those who have the power to understand It,
for It dwells in the heart of every one;
but It seems far to those whose mind is
covered by the clouds of sensuality and self-delusion.
It is within, because It is the innermost Soul of all creatures;
and It is without as the essence of the whole external universe,
infilling it like the all-pervading ether." – Isha Upanishad 5

INTRODUCTION

The following quotations on *Feeling and Human Evolution* and *The Fear of Opening* from the book *The Hathor Material* by Tom Kenyon and Virginia Essene are about the importance of being aware of feelings and emotion as keys toward healing and self-mastery. They are compiled here to support the practice of lightbody (merkaba) or Ka development for emotional and self-mastery, healing and stress management through *Merkaba Meditation, Distance Healing Technique, Sun gazing* and *Dr. Johanna Budwig's Diet Protocol* which altogether will be elaborated in the further pages of this book.

This book's goal besides building the *Ka* or *pranic body life-force* to birth a *Sahhu* or an *immortal golden lightbody* is to offer readers an effective how-to-technique to manage emotional stress, the main cause of disease, in their daily lives and spiritually awaken when emotional stress is cleared, released and stabilized. Basically, the emotional mastery technique is simply connecting your awareness (attention) to the pranic tube – chong mai (neutral core) in the center of the body according to Chinese Medical Qigong Therapy – and intentionally allowing the prana or Qi from the Sun above and Earth below to flow in the pranic tube together with *opening the heart to unconditional love* and activating the Ka or Merkaba. Doing this practice will provide a fast, safe way to stabilize your chaotic emotions such anger or fear.

According to the Hathor Material, "So practice this technique in the day-to-day situations in which you find yourself. Use it in situations where you may previously have become frustrated or angry situations that may have triggered situations, situations that brought up fear. Yes, practice this technique and you will create an amazing sense of stability and groundedness in a way you may never have experienced before. From this place of power you have the option of moving into a greater choice of alternative responses to a situation, because you will not be swayed by emotions in the past.

Being conscious of this energy core (pranic tube) that extends through your body creates a way for you to stabilize your subtle bodies, stabilize your magnetic and electromagnetic fields, and stabilize the emotional body so that you find yourself responding to difficult situations from a place of balance. It will be a remarkable shift for some of you who feel as if you are frequently buffeted by chaotic emotions and your seesaw reactions to life's situations. Please note that mastery of the emotional body is not the same as suppression of emotion. The goal is to feel emotion deeply and fully in a balanced and integrated manner. Suppressing (denying) feelings and emotions will not serve you."

"If you are able to balance yourself through the method of connecting to the pranic tube and allowing the pranic flow to be continuous, then you can stabilize yourself in situations that might otherwise throw you off center, so to speak. The exercises have to be practiced on a regular basis until you know, beyond a shadow of a doubt, that you have mastered them!

Relatively few humans living in highly technologically developed countries have studied yogic techniques and other meditative practices well enough to claim that they have emotional fields under adverse circumstances – which is why we have come forth with this information. We believe these exercises provide a fast, safe way to assist humans to achieve greater consciousness in everyday living. Please try them with personal commitment and persistence until you know they work for you as an energetic reality."

"Mastery of the emotional body, however, is not the same as control. The goal is not to suppress the emotional body, but to stabilize it. And energetics are definitely part of this, because Earth reality is much a school for learning to master one's emotions without suppressing or controlling them. One of the things that beings definitely come to this planet to learn is to ride the energy of emotion in a masterful way."

Where awareness (attention) goes, energy flows.
Where energy flows, awareness follows.

The Taoist saying "Where awareness (attention) goes, energy flows," is an important first principle behind the Hathor's technique to stabilize your chaotic emotion: connecting your awareness (attention) to the pranic tube and grounding it to the center of Mother Earth works to stabilize your emotions and feelings because the process stabilizes your subtle bodies, stabilizes your magnetic and electromagnetic fields, and stabilizes the emotional body so that you find yourself responding rather than reacting to emotional situations such as fear or anger from a place of balance.

The Taoist second saying "Where energy flows, awareness follows," is an important second principle behind the Hathor's technique of connecting to the pranic tube and opening your heart to unconditional love because what you are doing is expanding your awareness to include this energy channel or pranic tube and into the heart – the Great Transformer or Central Sun – which connects to the celestial realm of higher vibratory frequency, and to the terrestrial energies of the Earth.

To add more power to this practice of connecting your awareness to you pranic tube is chanting with gratitude four times the Hathor's mantra – EL-KA-LEEM-OM – which connects you to each of the Four Sacred Elements. "EL" is Earth; "KA" is fire(Sun); "LEEM" is water; and "OM" is space or air. These four constitute a vibrational continuum. It is possible to chant the sounds of these elements and enter the archetypal realms in which they exist.

According to the Hathors, "It is as if these sounds open the door of perceptions and allow you to move into the resonant field of consciousness where the archetypal realm of the elements are alive. Indeed, entering into that realm and staying there for a while enables you to shift consciousness and perception in such a way that you sense the profundity of the physical world and also its place within the continuum of consciousness."

With thanks and acknowledgements to Ricardo's guide, the Hathors, to Tom Kenyon and Virginia Essene, authors of the *Hathor Material,* to Dr. Candace Pert's *Molecules of Emotion,* to my Holographic Sound Healing teacher Paul Hubbert, to my Merkaba teacher Alton Kamadon, to Dr. Nelie Johnson's *You Hold the Keys to Your Healing,* Renee Brodie's *Crystal Bowls,* to Dr. Richard Gerber's *Vibrational Medicine, to* Katrina Raphaell's *Crystalline Transmission,* to Drunvalo Melchizedek's *Living in the Heart,* to Swami Lakshmanjoo's *Shiva Sutras, to* Dr. Johanna Budwig's *Diet for Cancer and Chronic Diseases, to* Lothar Hirneise' *Quotations on Cancer and Dr. Budwig's Oil-Protein diet, to* Udo Erasmus' *Fats that Heal and Fats that Kill, Hira Ratan Manek's Sun Gazing,* and *to my daughter* Anne Serrano's foreword, *my student, proof reader critic.*

Ricardo B Serrano, R.Ac.
http://www.qigongmastery.ca

Quotations on Feeling and Human Evolution

True feelings are neither positive nor negative. They are simply neutral reports, a kind of barometer about what is happening in your own energy-responsive, energy-attuned world.

Your feeling nature is an attribute of your emotional body which is closely related to the Ka. The emotional body is a field of energy that surrounds and interpenetrates your physical body. When something activates the emotional body it begins to vibrate in specific ratios setting off "energy flows" which stream around and through the physical body. If these flows are strong enough (i.e., when a strong feeling/emotional reaction occurs), these flows can be physically felt within the tissues of the body itself – thus the stronger the feeling response the stronger the physical sensation. One of the keys to the ascension process, from an energetic standpoint, is to allow your energy fields to open and move freely. The ability to move energy and to master positive movement of that energy comes from the cultivation of your feeling nature.

Your emotions have an effect on health which is being more clearly demonstrated and documented in your sciences.

Allowing the energy of unconditional acceptance and love to move through the emotional body activates a process of profound healing and balance.

When you resist feelings or emotions, your emotional body cannot vibrate properly and it "freezes" or locks-up. When it is not able to move or vibrate properly, you become less aware mentally and your thoughts get fuzzy, unclear and muddled.

The life situations that arise today on your planet and the emotions they generate are actually the initiatory phases of higher consciousness leading to ascension and mastery.

The key is allowing yourself to be aware of your feelings and emotional responses to situations so they can be noticed and balanced. Because the emotional body and the Ka are energetically connected, by strengthening your Ka and by bringing your emotions and feelings into full and positive awareness, you greatly accelerate your own evolution.

With the exception of the physical body, the various other interpenetrating fields are like luminous egg-shaped fields of light and they are imbedded in each other. The Ka is actually a complex field of energy. Its primary form is similar to that of the physical body though slightly larger. This is why it is called the "etheric or spiritual twin" in Egyptian alchemy. The early Egyptians understood its nature and relationship to the physical form. Indeed, the Ka can move about and even bi-locate (in which a person appears to be in two places at the same time). The Ka also has an auric field of energy around it which we call the pranic body.

When we refer to the Ka we often mean both its primary form and its auric field. This field is egg-shaped, much like the other fields, and can get quite large as a person moves upward in consciousness. *This auric field around the Ka can ignite at a certain moment in the upward movement of ascension and become a field of intense golden light.* The early Egyptians referred to this as the "*Sahhu*" or glorious spiritual body.

Generally speaking, for most people, the pranic body extends from a few inches to several feet from the physical body. The emotional body is the next body and is slightly larger than the pranic body (Ka). The mental body is slightly larger still because it holds memory holographically in space around the physical body. From there, the astral body is actually a subtler sheath that is slightly larger, just barely larger than the mental body. Beyond the astral body is the next luminous egg-shaped field which we call the etheric body. Finally the causal body, the least dense of all, is the point of light above the other luminous eggs. All of these subtle bodies emit light and sound.

A being such as Jesus or an Avatar will have fields that extend for several miles and in some cases hundreds of miles. In terms of the etheric body of one who has fully ascended, the etheric body includes all of the known universes within itself. So it has expanded to include all levels, all information, all knowledge! Omniscience is available to anyone at that level for they have actually merged their bodies with the universal body. In regards to the smallest-sized field possible, that would be the Ka's auric field or pranic body during times of illness. In cases of extreme illness, the Ka's vitality is lowered and the field shrinks. It can literally pull into the body, so that there is no pranic force around, or at the surface of the body at all.

Hathor
EL-KA-LEEM-OM

From our understanding, this is the very point. The energetic thing is to realize that the emotional body and the Ka are very close. So what happens when fear occurs is that the emotional body begins to vibrate very fast, and, if you identify with the emotion of fear, then the fear becomes amplified. Depending on how strong the fear pattern is, it may be possible to talk yourself out of feeling fearful. But when the emotional body vibrates in a full-fledged attack of fear, it will override the mental body and you won't be able to think your way out of the situation. You will just be paralyzed with fear.

But, if one goes to the Ka, one can transmute the fear very quickly. The solution goes back to the central column or pranic tube. When you experience an intense, difficult emotion or feeling, first identify where in the body it's located because you'll need that reference point. Then you go to the Ka, the pranic tube, and hold your awareness in the center of the tube that goes right through the middle of the body. In other words, your awareness shifts to the Ka. What will happen is that the emotional body will begin to shift, and as the vibration of fear begins to oscillate with the stability of the pranic tube, the fear will become more and more subtle, more manageable.

As an analogy, consider those toys you call tops which children play with and spin. Tops have a central column of energy – though it's invisible – that runs up through the middle. That's its center of gravity, its center of balance, actually. As long as the top is spinning with enough speed it will stay upright. But as it loses speed, it will start to wobble, become unbalanced and fall over.

That's very similar to the dynamic between the Ka and the emotional body when you experience a negative emotional response to something – you can have a feeling that you are literally out of balance, can't you? This happens when the emotional body is spinning and vibrating in a resonance that is out of balance. However, if you locate where that sensation is in the body and at the same time link your awareness to the pranic tube, your emotional body will come back into balance very quickly.

As long as the Ka is strong, it can ameliorate this other situation of fear. If the person is not full of good energy at the Ka level, then that causes debilitating conditions.

This is why it's critical to feel and maintain our energy level, then, because Christ Jesus once said that humans lose their mastery at the emotional level.

So it is absolutely vital to keep the Ka energy strong.

Ka (Merkaba)

Attending to the Ka on a daily basis becomes part of one's daily life. It is simply part of the human equation for health and higher consciousness.

As important as eating. Yes. Understand that the Ka is the essential fundamental body. *The Ka can exist – even after the physical body dies – for a certain period of time which can be as much as several thousand years*. Some of the ancient practices in Egypt were to activate the Ka so that one survives one's death consciously until one was able to move with full awareness and consciousness up into the higher bodies and realms of awareness.

Your potential is much higher when you develop the Ka, because the Ka vibrates much faster than any of the bodies – with the exception of the etheric and the causal. The Ka supplies the building blocks, if you will, at the subtle realm for the actual physical body, the actual cells. It supplies the energies and the architecture for the mental body and the emotional body and it also sustains the astral body. If you were to remove the Ka, those subtle bodies will dissolve. If you were to dissolve the physical body, the mental body and the astral body, but the Ka was still strong, the Ka would remain. So the Ka is like a master over the lower bodies, if you think of it this way.

The other bodies become as servants to the Ka, the pranic body, and the life-force. Then if one takes that life-force and directs it to the higher bodies in service to the etheric. the causal, the monad, the Source of all that is – then one has a truly powerful alchemy!

We just want to be sure that it is clear to the reader how to use the Ka to balance uncomfortable emotion in the way we have just described. The first is step is for the reader to begin to sense where they feel different feelings in their physical bodies. The second step is to rebalance that emotional energy by using the pranic tube, which we clarified previously as a necessary skill.

So what we say is that the movement of energy through the emotional body is a positive thing because it is how you are going through the initiatory process of your life. However, the habit of humans to label feeling responses to situations as good, bad, uncomfortable, difficult, and so forth, does not serve them. Contrarily, it often causes them to resist things they find uncomfortable. Now, we are not saying that the process itself of labeling and identifying the feeling patterns is wrong. But we are saying that, of the result of labeling causes you to clamp down and prevent yourself from moving through an emotional experience, then that is anti-evolutionary – because it locks-up and "freezes" the energy bodies.

It blocks; it stops; it becomes rigid. Then the Ka has to respond and tends to get jammed as well, depending on how intense the emotional response is. When the Ka freezes up, prana does not flow into that area of the body where the emotional pattern is held. So if that emotional pattern tends to be fear and is held in the kidneys, for example, the prana cannot flow into the kidneys; and you may eventually have a problem on the physical level of the kidneys.

Quotations on the Fear of Opening

Humans, from our experience, are a fascinating group of beings for many reasons. One aspect that we find most intriguing is that what they want most, they fear the most. So opening into a greater reality – greater emotional freedom, greater spiritual awareness – is both a yearning and a fear. This fear of opening to heart love is rooted in many different causes, some of which, quite frankly, develop from how you have been raised as children.

We have chosen to communicate our thoughts about humans' fear of opening to love, because from our perspective the doorway to accelerated evolution and growth lies in what you would call "feelings." We note that as humans open up to deeper feelings there is also a powerful tendency for many people to hold back, to fear that very process of experiencing deep, powerful feelings. For it is through this process of opening to feeling that your greatest strides in evolution and in awareness will occur.

Please remember that the different subtle bodies resonate to different specific frequencies. As stated earlier, the emotional body is very connected to the Ka. The Ka, your pranic body – the life-force itself – and emotional body are very closely intertwined! If you allow yourself to experience deep feelings, then you are allowing the Ka to vibrate at a faster rate. By this we do not mean becoming hysterical, over-volatile, or over-emotional. We simply mean that the *capacity to feel deeply, whether it is expressed or not, allows the Ka to vibrate at a faster rate.*

The organization of the chakras is related to what you call feeling levels. And as the energies move into the heart chakra, the "Great Transformer" at the center of the chest, there is a movement of this feeling energy into its greatest tonality or acutely tuned to frequencies. The heart area is also the mid-point between the lower and the upper chakras which is why many refer to it as the "Great Transformer." It is the Central Sun of the body and it is the cantilever from which all movement takes place energetically into wholeness and into higher states of consciousness. The heart center is "petal-like," but all the different chakras literally have an energetic structure in the subtle realm that is much like a flower. Whenever the flower of the heart opens, there is an increase in feelings. So as one experiences more feeling, the petals of the heart open and extend themselves. As one feels less and less emotion – becoming more withdrawn and less attuned to one's own feeling – these petals tend to close up.

Feelings give you a very clear barometer, and emotions give you a very clear feedback about what you are honestly experiencing and telling yourself about the experience. If you allow yourself to experience these with openness and acceptance, these deep feelings will create, in you, greater awareness. Simply stated, *the emotion and feeling energies that move through you are fuel for the fires of transmutation.*

Some of the fears of opening to feelings have to do with the actual energetics – for when the subtle bodies begin to open, real physical sensation moves through the physical body. For the uninformed, this can be alarming because one knows and feels that something profound is happening, something earth-shaking! Depending on the individual's personality and the decisions they have made about reality and their place in it, such an opening can actually be terrifying. And yet the opening into the greater space of one's own being, into a greater awareness and a greater sense of freedom and fluidity, is your birthright. This spiritual birthright is what your bodies are evolving to, if you will just allow the process to proceed.

Yes, the fear of opening comes from many levels so complex that we could spend the entire book discussing these complexities. Therefore, we now give you a most simple exercise that will allow the heart center to open and permit you to experience a greater deeper depth of feeling. Like all other tools we have given, it may seem deceptively simple, but we have found that the most powerful things in life are often the most simple in nature, the easiest to apply.

Moving your awareness into the pranic tube, you breathe into the tube the heavenly and earthly energy and into the heart center or chakra, and you visualize a flower opening as you exhale. The goal is to feel the energy of the heart opening like petals on a flower and feeling the flower opening larger and larger so that the petals open as wide as your body. Then let the petals extend further and further, as far as you are comfortable in opening.

What you are doing in this simple exercise is to activate both the emotional body and the Ka. As the emotional body becomes activated, it sets up a resonance with the pranic body, the Ka, and as you feel the heart opening, you are literally creating an electromagnetic opening in the heart! Once this happens you will feel physical sensations and movements of energy in a gentle way so that your personality can become more accustomed to the feeling of being open. It's simply a matter of becoming accustomed to the feeling of being open-hearted instead of being closed down. As you practice this simple method over a short period of time, you will find your ability to open the heart greatly increasing and your fear of opening greatly decreasing. This is the simplification of something extremely complex.

We hope you will continue to develop the ability to imagine a flower in the center of your chest, its petals opening, because as you imagine the petals of a flower opening like a blossom, the heart center will respond accordingly. You see, there is a connection, an energetic connection. Between what is held in the mental and emotional bodies. So as you hold the image of this flower, opening in your imagination, in your mind if you will, it is creating a resonance with the subtle structure of what you would call the heart chakra, allowing the heart chakra to begin to open.

This simple exercise of opening an imaginary flower in the center of the chest can do wonders for any lingering reluctance to open. It can assist you to become more sensitive to feeling your own great depths – and as we have said again and again, *"Feeling is the fuel for transmutation and the food for evolution and growth."*

For us, the essential balance point is the universal stream of love that is literally palpable and flows through all levels of existence. It is a resonance that reflects in our emotion as unconditional acceptance, unconditional love. So it is our desire to achieve this alignment, this balance point, if you will, in all life experiences. Those experiences where we may find it a challenge are our own growth points, just as they are for you. Being in that resonance of acceptance leads one to understand another's suffering, which is compassion.

For us, therefore, the central pivotal point is achieving the vibratory field of high coherency, unconditional love and unconditional acceptance. To live our lives through, and in, that vibratory field allows us to move up the ascending spiral of consciousness. Then we can assist others who may not be in that vibratory field of love, who may not love themselves, or may be actively hurting themselves or another. We have found that being in that vibratory field (love) and experiencing all situations from that positive feeling state has been the greatest catalyst for our own evolution.

- Excerpts from *The Hathor Material* by Tom Kenyon & Virginia Essene, 1996.

CONCLUSION

CONCLUDING NOTE by Ricardo B Serrano, R.Ac.: From my experience as an Omkabah Heart Lightbody Facilitator, emotional mastery is possible and a necessary practice of the Omkabah Lightbody Activation. By centering your awareness to your pranic tube and grounding it to the earth during emotional turmoils such as anger or fear, you become stabilized. And together with opening your heart to unconditional love of the Father Sun Source and Mother Earth through Ka or Merkaba activation, are invaluable spiritual tools – keys to healing and self-mastery – to build the *Sahhu* or the *immortal golden lightbody*.

In August 2001 in a Holographic Sound Healing workshop with Paul Hubbert, I became conscious of these Beings around me who were assisting me with my own and others' sound and emotional work. I have come to know and remember these Beings as the Hathors, *the Masters of Sound and Love*, who work directly with the feeling nature, assisting all who come into their sphere of influence to enter higher levels of insight and evolution.

They are like Inter Dimensional big brothers and sisters to us, residing in the higher dimensions. They have been with us for thousands and thousands of years and exhibited a very strong influence in the earlier days of Egypt.

According to the Hathors, "It has been said that the body is the temple of God. We agree that your body is a sacred temple for it is the space in which the four consciousness of earth, fire, water and air (space) offer themselves to you in service.

We see Earth as a sacred space, an outpicturing of the Sacred Elements of the archetypal realm of consciousness itself. We see Earth being as close to God as any other realm, for the continuum is whole. Whether one experiences oneself as close to divinity or separated from it, has nothing to do with whether one is on Earth, embodied or not. One's view is something that is held in personal consciousness. It is possible to be in deep communion with the Divine, to feel completely at home in consciousness, and still be embodied. It is not necessary to leave Earth in order to go "home," for home is a state of consciousness, a state of connectedness generated from within yourself."

"We would recommend that you frequently enter into nature and spend time with the natural elements, for they are the outpicturing of the archetypal patterns. Don't insulate yourselves from the air, the Sun (fire) and the other elements. Embrace them. Appreciate them. Allow your awareness and consciousness to become attuned to the Four Sacred Elements. Chant the names of the elements – EL-KA-LEEM-OM – in a state of reverence and an inner world will open up to you far beyond your imagination. As you enter this inner world, the archetypal world of the elements, you will find a place where you are more deeply connected to the natural world around you and you will see the world with new eyes. You will see and clearly understand that the Earth itself is a sacred temple, and wherever you go – God is."

The main thing to remember is to always connect your awareness to your pranic tube and the *Ka* or Merkaba lightbody around you before chanting the sacred mantra – EL-KA-LEEM-OM – not only to heal and to stabilize your emotions, but also to expand your awareness and return home, *by feeling the emotion of love within the sacred space of your heart that connects you to God consciousness*.

According to the Hathors, "Finally, we would say to you that you hold the keys to your own liberation, to your enlightenment, to your own upliftment. These keys are obtained through the power of your awareness, your ability to make choices, and the law of vibration and resonance. If your consciousness resonates with the highest of the high, you will experience life in an exalted celestial way. If you experience your life through the vibration of conflict and greed and constricted awareness then you will experience life as a kind of hell. All of these domains and realms exist simultaneously and can be activated by you at any moment. In fact, they are activated by you every moment of your life through the act of choice.

While living your life in service to the greater life, to the evolution of consciousness as it expresses through you, you assure yourself a secure footing on the stairway that leads to the heavenly realms. Whatever choice you make, acknowledge your mastery and your freedom to express it. To those of you who have already chosen, or who now choose to serve life and the growth of consciousness as it expresses through you and all beings, we welcome you as brothers and sisters on the journey. So be it."

"The true meaning of holy goes back to the concept of wholeness, to make whole. So to make whole is to do holy work – the sacred task of unifying the great Universe in awareness. This is done from human to human or sometimes human to pets, animals, plants and other life-forms. Essentially it's done from being to being. By acknowledging within yourself that each being you meet has value, you serve life. You may not know who they are, their history, or what they believe, but they are part of life and so you acknowledge them. If you hold that intent in your energy field, love and acceptance get communicated to them. And that is serving life.

"We would say in final closing that within you, the human, is a great mystery waiting to unfold itself and to bedazzle you. All that is needed is the touch of love. So love yourself, love others. It is that simple. So be it through all time and all space."

The following articles will elaborate on the fundamental knowledge and processes behind the *Merkaba Meditation Procedure, Distance Healing Technique and Sun Gazing* together with Qigong that build your *Sahhu* or *immortal golden lightbody: Tube Torus, Morphic Resonance, Pantheism, Pranic Tube, Who the Hathors are, Molecules of Emotion, Vibrational Medicine, Holograms and Spiritual Healing, Holographic Sound Healing, Crystal Bowls, Ka of the Sun, Hymns to the Sun, Sun's Solar Ka Body, Medicines of Light*, the *Five Agreements, Sacred Space of the Heart, The Sahhu or Immortal Golden Lightbody and Its Soul Powers, Sun Yoga and Its Healing and Enlightenment Aspects,* and *Enlightenment Qigong Forms for Returning to Oneness*.

Dr. Budwig's *Diet for Cancer and Chronic Diseases* is also included to provide readers with cancer and chronic diseases an effective dietary protocol they can use together with the emotional stress healing and lightbody activation techniques to build the *Ka* pranic body, *Qi* and *Jing* which are all taught in this book.

Your Pranic Tube, Tube Torus and Ka

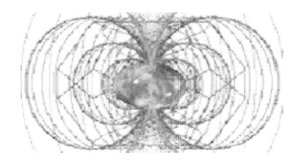

All living things have an electromagnetic field around them, as do our physical bodies. Therefore, we recognize that the human body is a bipolar magnet with a central column we will refer to as pranic tube (chong mai). Three dimensionally, all bipolar magnets emit a field resembling a donut-like shape called a **Tube Torus**. This field moves around our body activated or expanded through the Omkabah Heart Lightbody Activation – rotate to gather, draw in, and condense heaven, earth and cosmic energies into the pranic tube within the spiralling Tube Torus as illustrated above -- is in a spiralling motion surrounding our Ka pranic body with physical, mental, spiritual bodies and higher chakras to manifest ascension or expansion of consciousness into infinity.

The chi or energy in the center of the body is the "*core energy*" (chong chi) along the neutral core (*chong mai*) in the center of the body. The core energy, chong chi, links and harmonizes the earth's subtle bodies to both the physical heavens (planets, sun, moon, stars) and our energy bodies, thus, harmony among heaven, man and earth. When you guide the core energy along the three tan tiens, dantian, heart and niwuan (center of the head), you build the immortal spirit body.

In recognizing ourselves as an energy system, to optimally sustain and perpetuate healthy life, it is of the utmost importance to pay attention to the Energy Field known as the **Ka (our pranic body)**.

As we move up the ascension spiral, our system requires more and more life force energy, which is generated through the **Ka (our pranic body)** into the emotional and physical bodies. This is sourced from the God Source, I AM consciousness, Earth Heart, appearing as the Oversoul Chakras now residing within the body.

Building the **Ka** is crucial to the process of raising your vibration in preparation for consciousness expansion or ascension.

By deliberately causing the **Ka** to intensify and radiate into the physical and emotional bodies via the *Layooesh* (pranic tube) in the Omkabah Heart Lightbody Activation, in a manner of speaking, force feeding yourself with life force energy, you begin the life rejuvenation process and prepare yourself for ascension or consciousness expansion.

The Human as an Energy System

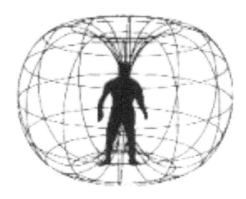

Your human body is a bipolar magnet with its central column sometimes referred to as the *central channel, the middle column, the pranic tube*, or the *antakarana* by various ancient traditions. All bipolar magnets, as your science has uncovered, emit a field that three-dimensionally resembles a donut-like shape called a "tube torus."

Going right down through the middle of the tube, the middle of this donut-like shape , is a channel of energy. This is actually the central column of the magnetic field that is emitted by the physical body. So this central column is the middle conduit, if you will, of an electromagnetic field that is the basis of life. In their esoteric understanding, many different cultures have touched upon and developed techniques involving this central column or pranic tube, as it is sometimes called.

Therefore, in terms of yourself as an energy system, the key central field to turn your attention to, from our understanding, is the Ka – the pranic body. How you draw in or do not draw in life-force (prana) determines how much energy is available to your organs and bodily systems. The Ka determines the clarity, the power, and the impact of your thought; and it also determines the quality of your emotion. If the Ka is disturbed then the other fields are disturbed – the physical body operates at a lesser level of energy, thought is diminished and emotions become perturbed. Then how do you bring more prana into the Ka so that it radiates out into the physical galaxy of your body and into the other subtle bodies, as well? This is the central question that we would now wish to answer.

The key lies in the pranic tube that extends down through the center of your body. This pranic tube roughly corresponds to a pathway that the yogis, in your tradition of this planet, called the "*sushumna*." The *sushumna* is the pathway by which the kundalini energy or life-force rises from the base of the spine, up through the various energy centers of the body (the chakras), into the head center.

Here it meets the crown and opens consciousness to what would be termed "cosmic consciousness" or the connection to All That Is – a very highly elevated state of consciousness! Although the energy of the life-force moves up through this pathway called the *sushumna*, if you do physical dissection of the body, you will not find it. It is a subtle energy. But it exists. It is as real as anything else in your world except that it is at a frequency domain that is outside the one percent of reality that you can perceive through the senses. However, the pranic tube, unlike the *sushumna*, does not follow the path of the spine, but forms a straight line from

the crown (at the top of the head) down through the perineum (a point midway between the genitals and anus).

This pranic tube actually extends into the Earth. Depending upon the development of your consciousness, it will either be connected just lightly above the Earth's surface, connected down below it just a few inches, or it can connect down to the very core of the Earth itself. This pranic tube also extends above the head and can go up several feet or several thousand miles, again depending upon the state of consciousness of the being. Generally speaking, if you touch your thumb and second finger together and make a circle, your pranic tube will be about the size of that circle. It does not bend with the spine. It extends, we can safely say in the way that we will be working with you, from the top of the head down through the perineum. This pranic tube focus is the primary method we would utilize with you in developing your capacity to activate the Ka, to increase the flow of prana throughout the physical body.

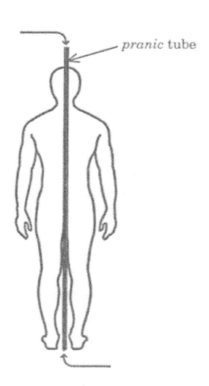

pranic tube

Understanding the laws and principles of the art and science of Merkaba Meditation – Omkabah Heart Lightbody Activation is the first step in becoming its Master.

Morphic Resonance

I would add that every time we expand the meridians and subtle energy fields by drawing Qi life force from the morphic fields of heaven, sun, moon and earth into our pranic body through the Omkabah Heart Lightbody Activation, we create morphic resonance with Spirit via the faculty of clairvoyance -- psychical transmission and reception of information and energy through space and time.

According to Dr. Rupert Sheldrake, "The extended mind resembles the traditional idea of the soul pervading and animating the body. But I think it is most helpful today to interpret this concept in terms of fields. The body is itself organized and pervaded by fields. As well as electromagnetic, gravitational, and quantum matter fields, morphogenetic fields shape its development and maintain its form. Behavioural, mental, and social fields underlie behaviour and mental life. According to the hypothesis of formative causation, morphogenetic, behavioural, mental, and social fields are different kinds of morphic fields, containing an inherent memory both from an individual's own past, and a collective memory from countless other people who have gone before.

Although I prefer to think of the fields of phantoms as morphic fields, the hypothesis I propose testing here is more general. I am not at present concerned with the specific feature of morphic fields, namely their habitual nature, shaped by morphic resonance. I am exploring the more general idea of fields as organizing patterns in space and time. I propose that these fields are located just where the phantoms seem to be. These fields can extend beyond the flesh-and-blood body, projecting beyond the stump."

Therefore, an individual who is regularly practicing the Omkabah Heart Lightbody Activation will receive the same encodings and energy from the ascended Masters, devoted Masters or practitioners of these practices who are radiating these encodings through morphic resonance.

Pantheism

"The independent state of supreme consciousness is the reality of everything."
– Shiva Sutra 1.1

This first sutra, *caitanyamatma,* states that individual being is one with universal being. The reality of this whole universe is God consciousness. It is filled with God consciousness.

The independent state of consciousness is the *Self*. It is the *Self* of everything, because whatever exists in the world is the state of Lord Shiva. So Lord Shiva is found everywhere.

"This world is nothing but the blissful energy of the all-pervading consciousness of Lord Shiva. God and the individual are one, to realize this is the essence of Shaivism." - Swami Lakshmanjoo

NOTE by Ricardo B Serrano: I believe in the God concept **pantheism** – *God is everything and everything is God, the universe and nature are divine* or *Unity consciousness*: whenever I clairvoyantly see the auras (etheric bodies) of people and trees, and feel so much bliss from that experience; whenever I do Qi-healing or Distance Healing and the blissful feeling that accompanies it; and whenever I experience blissful transcendental Oneness during meditation and Qigong practices.

"Natural consciousness is the pure embodiment of Consciousness. It is Shiva. All of the thirty-six elements, from Shiva to earth, are created by that natural I-Consciousness. And not only are they created by that Consciousness, they also shine in that Consciousness. His creation is not outside of His nature, it exists in His own Self. He has created this whole universe in the cycle of His Consciousness. So, everything that exists resides in that Consciousness.

This must be your understanding. The creative energy which is attributed to Lord Shiva is not that energy of Lord Shiva that creates the universe outside of His Consciousness as we create outside of our consciousness. His creation is not insentient as our creations are.

This universe, which is created in His Consciousness, is dependent on that Consciousness. It is always dependent on that Consciousness. It cannot move outside of that Consciousness. It exists only when it is residing in His Consciousness. This is the way the creation of His universe takes place.

You must understand that this universe, which is created by the Lord of Consciousness, is one with that Creator Who is wholly self-luminous light with Consciousness.

If this created universe were to remain outside of Consciousness then it would not appear to anyone. It would not exist, just as the son of a barren woman or the milk of a bird do not exist. If we go in the depth of this understanding, we will see that there is a difference between these analogies. If this created universe were to remain outside of Consciousness, it would not appear to anyone because it would not exist at all. Actually only Consciousness exists. In this way, because this universe exists, it is one with Consciousness. In reality, nothing would exist if it were separate from this Consciousness. It is in this sense that we can say that the son of a barren woman or the milk of a bird are existing. They are existing because they are existing in Consciousness as long as they are residing in our thought. When it is in imagination it is existing in Consciousness. Ksemaraja is telling us that this universe is not outside of Consciousness. So, the son of a barren woman or the milk of a bird are not existing outside of Consciousness. We can think of them, so they are also existing inside of Consciousness.

The Consciousness of Lord Shiva is not overshadowed by this created world. The world cannot obscure Consciousness. On the contrary, Consciousness gives rise to the existence of this world.

This world is existing on the surface of Consciousness. So how could this world cover or conceal the nature of Consciousness? The truth is, this world gets its life from Consciousness. It is filled with the light of Consciousness. The universe can not conceal its life, which is Consciousness. If this universe could conceal the Consciousness of Lord Shiva, how would it exist? It would not – it would disappear." – Swami Lakshmanjoo

Source: *Self Realization in Kashmir Shaivism* by Swami Lakshmanjoo, p.57-58

Who The Hathors Are & Why They Have Come

According to Channelled Messages from the Hathors in Tom Kenyon and Virginia Essene's Hathor Material book, "We are the Hathors. We come in love and with the sounding of a new dream reality for your earth. If you are ready to build the new world, we invite you to join us on a journey of the mind and heart. We are your elder brothers and sisters. We have been with you for a very long period of your evolution on this planet. We were with you in eons past - even in the forgotten days before any trace of us is known in your present written history. Our own nature is energetic and interdimensional. We originally came from another universe by way of Sirius which is a portal to your Universe, and from Sirius we eventually proceeded to your solar system and the etheric realms of Venus.

In the past we have specifically worked with and through the Hathor fertility goddess of ancient Egypt. We also made contact with the Tibetan lamas in the formative period of Tibetan Buddhism. Thus, some of their unique techniques and practices about the use of sound come from our own lineage and our teachings with them. Although we have interacted with some of Earth's early cultures, we are an intergalactic civilization with outposts that span parts of your known Universe and beyond.

We are what you might term an ascended civilization – a group of beings existing at a specific vibratory field, even as you have an energy signature. It is simply that we vibrate at a faster rate than you. Nonetheless, we are all part of the mystery, part of the love that holds and binds all the universe together.

We have grown as you have grown, ascending to the One Source of all that is. We have grown in joy and through sorrow, as have you. We are, in terms of the vastness, a little higher on the spiral of awareness and consciousness than you are; therefore, we can offer you what we have learned as friends, mentors and fellow travelers on the path that leads back to remembrance of All That Is.

We are not saviors; we're not messianic. We wanted to clearly step out of that projection so that the reader understood that we were simply elder brothers and sisters offering our understanding and what we have learned. You may take it or leave it but we offer it freely. In our understanding, the belief that different alien intelligences are going to save you, and the belief that when you enter a photon belt you will magically be transformed, are just projection of human unconsciousness. The hope that someone or something will save you, that you will not have to make any changes in yourself, that you will not have to be responsible, is unrealistic.

The belief that you can stay in patterns of lethargy and unconsciousness, then take something or have something given to you that will transform you without any effort on your part, is sheer folly. It won't happen. Now, there may be alien intelligences that land, for they certainly exist, but those humans who count on others to bring in their ascension and elevation without any work on their part, are going to be very disappointed. **Ascension is a process of self-awareness and mastery on all levels** and it necessitates bringing all those levels of one's existence upward. That is how we see it and that is how we have done it for millennia.

By offering our aid, however, we do not wish to interfere with your other spiritual helpers and cosmic relationships in any way, nor with any religious beliefs, affiliations or organizations of help to you. Even so, there is a great deal we would like to share.

We know Sanat Kumara well for it was he who asked us to enter this Universe. As an Ascended Master, Sanat Kumara has taken on numerous responsibilities associated with the elevation of planet Earth and this solar system. He is working for the ascension, the evolution of consciousness in the solar system, as we are. "

According to *The Ancient Secret of The Flower of Life Volume 2 by Drunvalo Melchizedek*, "The Hathors were the main or primary mentors within the Left Eye of Horus Mystery School. Though they were not from Earth, in the ancient days they were always here to assist us in unfolding our consciousness. They loved us dearly, and still do. As our consciousness became more and more third-dimensional, we eventually could no longer see them or respond to their teachings. Only now, as we grow, are we beginning to see and communicate with them again. The Hathor race is a race of fourth-dimensional beings who come from Venus. You don't see them on the third-dimensional world of Venus, but if you tune to Venus on the fourth dimension, especially on the higher overtones, you'll find a vast culture there. They are the most intelligent consciousness in this solar system, and they function as the headquarters or central office for all life under our Sun. If you come into our solar system from the outside, you must check with Venus before proceeding.

The Hathors are beings of tremendous love. Their love is on a level of Christ consciousness. They use vocal sounds as their means of communicating and performing feats within their environment. They have amazing ears. They have almost no darkness to them at all; they're just light – pure, loving beings.

Hathors are very much like dolphins. Dolphins use sonar to do almost everything, and Hathors use their voices to do almost everything. We create machines to light or heat our houses, but the Hathors simply use sound through their voices.

The Hathors are about 10 – 16 feet tall. For a very, very long time they have helped people on Earth, almost always through their love and their incredible knowledge of sound. There's an initiation in Egypt where the sound of the ankh is created – this is one of the initiations in the Great Pyramid. It's a continuous sound that a Hathor makes, without stopping, for somewhere between half an hour to an hour. It is used primarily for healing the body or restoring balance in nature. It's like when we sound Om and have to breathe at the same time. The Hathors learned how to make a sound without stopping, breathing in through their nose, into their lungs and back out through their mouth continuously. Conducting this sound-of-the-ankh initiation ceremony was only one of the many things they would do for us to create balance. The Hathors were here on Earth helping mankind for thousands of years.

Breathing in and out at the same time and making a continuous sound without stopping is not unheard-of today. An Aborigine playing the didgeridoo uses circular breathing. He can make one tone nonstop for an hour by controlling the air flow into and out of his body. It's not that hard to learn, actually."

HOLOGRAPHIC SOUND HEALING

*In the beginning was the Word, and the Word was with God,
and the Word was God.* – John 1:1

Holographic Sound, as described by the Hathors, Masters of Sound and Love, is a merging of sound vibration with holographic energy, bringing sound to its true and natural state of being. Sound is holographic in nature but for the past several thousand years, has only been used in linear form because of our inability to hold its higher vibration. Through specific Holographic Sound Healing techniques, we are able to hold once again this higher vibration.

Holographic Sound Healing together with the Holographic Light Body Activation, through your *Sahhu* or *immortal golden lightbody,* will completely and exponentially amplify the vibration of sound and light body for healing, balancing, body rejuvenation, interdimensional travel, manifestation, ascension and much, much more as I have experienced it in my regular practice and clinical healing application.

If you have the opportunity to interact with the Hathors during holographic healing session through the core energy in your pranic tube, I would strongly encourage you to invite them. Their presence will be an experience you will surely not forget.

"The chakras or energy centers hold the patterning and govern all physical, emotional, mental, and energetic aspects of the body. Each organ and all parts of the body are represented and sourced through one or more of the chakras. All patterning for energetic, emotional, mental, emotional, and physical manifestations of our physical beingness, appear in the chakras. **The chakras are the energetic blueprint to Balance**. *Always remember there is always an emotional component to any physical manifestation*." – Paul Hubbert

For more information on Holographic Sound Healing , please review *Meditation and Qigong Mastery* book. Also visit www.holisticwebs.com/sound

Reasons to Address Your Stress

The stress hormones that trigger the fight-or-flight reaction caused by persistent stress over the long term pose serious threats to your health which is why you must address your stress.

Elevated levels of stress hormone cortisol lead to inflammatory conditions such as atherosclerosis. Cortisol suppresses the immune system and also lead to flare-ups of existing conditions such as ulcers, asthma, cold sores or eczema. Elevated levels of stress hormone adrenaline elevate both blood pressure and heart rate increasing your risk of heart attack or stroke.

The chemical changes created by stress can alter brain function and trigger anxiety and depression that produce chronic insomnia, obesity and substance abuse; affects cognitive function such as short and long term memory; and reduces sex drive leading to impotence and lower fertility.

Symptoms of persistent stress include anxious or negative thoughts or feelings, loss of concentration, frequent illness, changes in diet or sleep patterns, nervousness, chest pain, irritability, procastination, and feelings of isolation.

While stress produces many negative effects, they are reversible. In fact, stress can be managed and reduced by going with and being in the flow of all things using Merkaba activation, Qigong and other natural Oriental healing modalities to cultivate the Three Treasures. Not eating junk food high in *trans-fatty acid*, and eating nutritious food that is high in *essential fatty acid* (EFA) such as *flaxseed oil* and *fish oil* will assist nutritionally.

According to Qi Dao Master Lama Tantrapa, "Struggling against the flow of a night-dream is a sure way to turn it into a nightmare. Similarly, if you struggle against the flow of your daily life, you single-handedly turn your life into a nightmare. Going against the flow of things only exhausts your energy, takes a toll on your health, and wastes your time. As soon as you realize that life's challenges can be perceived as learning opportunities rather than problems, you will become less tense or "stressed-out" and find yourself in the flow of life. Being in the flow will empower you to live your dreams."

Our lives are filled with stress reflected by our mental attitude and emotional experience. Because of our own ignorance, we look for love, happiness, peace, joy and contentment outside where they are not. Ka or Merkaba meditation elaborated in this book is a simple and direct means to experience within you an ocean of love, peace, joy, happiness and well-being in a continuous basis.

Quotations from book *Molecules of Emotion*
by Dr. Candace Pert, PhD

"Western medicine may say "it is all in your head." The paradigm has got to shift. Even if it was entirely mental, thinking it's all in your head shows no awareness of the new research, suggesting the consciousness is a body-mind wide phenomenon." – Dr. Candace Pert

The mind is not just in the brain – it is also in the body. The vehicle that the mind and body use to communicate with each other is the chemistry of emotion. The chemicals in question are molecules, short chains of amino acids called peptides and receptors, that she believes to be the "biochemical correlate of emotion." The peptides can be found in your brain, but also in your stomach, your muscles, your glands and all your major organs, sending messages back and forth. After decades of research, Dr. Pert is finally able to make clear how emotion creates the bridge between mind and body.

Dr. Pert's striking conclusion that it is our emotions and their biological components that establish the crucial link between mind and body does not, however, serve to repudiate modern medicine's gains; rather, her findings complement existing techniques by offering a new scientific understanding of the power of our minds and our feelings to affect our health and well-being.

Dr. Pert explains that perception and awareness play a vital part in health and longevity. She is able to explain how her research bridges the mind and body gap that is sadly prevalent in modern traditional medicine. Her views on mind-body cellular communication mesh well with the concepts of energy held by many alternative therapies, and she is now, not surprisingly, a popular lecturer on the wellness circuit. Her book describes an eight-part program for a healthy lifestyle, and she has appended an extensive list of alternative medicine resources. For all of those who have sought out complementary medicine, this book will confirm what you have long suspected: that alternative approaches to health do work. Dr. Pert explains why.

The scientific basis of the components of the molecules of emotion has basically two parts: The receptors that receive the smaller molecule, kind of into themselves on the surfaces of self. The other half is the ligand, the small molecule that binds to the receptors. These smaller molecules can be drugs, hormones, or other chemicals – chemicals made from within, many of which are peptides in their structure. These are all over, not just the brain but different parts of the body, including the heart and the vessels around the heart.

Do we treat physical conditions from an emotional point of view or vice versa? Dr. Pert says, "I honestly cannot differentiate the physical from the mental, vice versa. The answer is you simultaneously do both, because they're flip sides of the same thing... I think a key word is balance, but I do feel that the meditation if possible twice a day in some kind of ritualized and not free-form form could be the cornerstone of a fitness program, along with exercise, which many studies have shown is the critical anti-aging variable in all kinds of animals and human beings." www.candacepert.com

"What causes people to consume legal and illegal drugs – one of the central problems in our society, I believe – is emotions that are unhealed, cut off, not processed and integrated or released. Trauma and stress continually lodged at the level of the receptor block nerve pathways and interrupt the smooth flow of information chemicals, a physiological condition we experience as stuck or unhealed emotions: chronic sadness, fear, frustration, anger. Reaching for that drink or cigarette or joint is usually precipitated by some disturbing and unacceptable feeling that we don't know how to deal with, and so we get rid of it in ways we know "work." The frustrated cigarette smoker, the depressed alcohol drinker, the hyper marijuana smoker – what if we stopped and checked in with our feelings to ask ourselves what emotions are present before using an artificial substance to alter our mood? If we can bring this level of awareness to our habitual use of substances, then we have a chance, a possibility, of making another choice. By continually ignoring feelings, we have none. Perhaps we'll find that it's a matter of a communication that needs to happen, a feeling that needs to be expressed, a need satisfied, a problem solved – all potential actions to get our own endogenous juices flowing for a natural, peptidergic "feel good" state. Or it could simply be that movement, in the form of exercise or a walk, could shift our mood."

"I had read The Relaxation Response, Herbert Benson's first book written in the seventies, in which he attributed meditation's power to an alternation of the nervous system from sympathetic to parasympathetic pathways. But with the knowledge of the body wide psychosomatic network, I was beginning to think of disease-related stress in terms of an information overload, a condition in which the mind-body network is so taxed by unprocessed sensory input in the form of suppressed trauma or undigested emotions that it has become bogged down and cannot flow freely, sometimes even working against itself, at cross-purposes... When stress prevents the molecules of emotion from flowing freely where needed, the largely autonomic processes that are regulated by peptide flow, such as breathing, blood flow, immunity, digestion, and elimination, collapse down to a few simple feedback loop and upset the normal healing response. Meditation, by allowing long-buried thoughts and feelings to surface, is a way of getting the peptides flowing again, returning the body, and the emotions, to health."

"My research has shown me that when emotions are expressed – which is to say that the biochemicals that are the substrate of emotion are flowing freely – all systems are united and made whole. When emotions are repressed, denied, not allowed to be whatever they may be, our network pathways get blocked, stopping the flow of the vital feel-good, unifying chemicals that run both our biology and our behavior. This, I believe, is the state of unhealed feeling we want so desperately to escape from. Drugs, legal and illegal, are further interrupting the many feedback loops that allow the psychosomatic network to function in a natural, balanced way, and therefore setting up conditions for somatic as well as mental disorders."

"It is my belief that this mysterious energy (Qi) is actually the free flow of information carried by the biochemicals of emotion, the neuropeptides and their receptors.

When stored or blocked emotions are released through touch or other physical methods, there is a clearing of our internal pathways, which we experience as energy. Free of western dualism that insists on disanimated flesh, healers from various Eastern and alternative modalities can literally see the mind in the body, where it does indeed exist, and are adepts at techniques that can get it unstuck if necessary. In fact, almost every other culture but ours recognizes the role played by some kind of emotional energy release, or catharsis, in healing.

Approaches that manipulate this kind of energy are almost unanimously rejected by most of Western medicine, with the possible exception of acupuncture, a discipline still looked on with suspicion."

"The emotions are a key element in self-care because they allow us to enter into the bodymind's conversation. By getting in touch with our emotions, both by listening to them and by directing them through the psychosomatic network, we gain access to the healing wisdom that is everyone's natural biological right.

And how do we do this? First by acknowledging and claiming all our feelings, not just the so-called positive ones. Anger, grief, fear – these emotional experiences are not negative in themselves; in fact, they are vital for survival. We need anger to define boundaries, grief to deal with our losses, and fear to protect ourselves from danger. It's only when these feelings are denied, so that they cannot be easily and rapidly processed through the system and released, that the situation becomes toxic. And the more we deny them, the greater the ultimate toxicity, which often takes the form of an explosive release of pent-up emotion. That's when emotion can becoming damaging to both oneself and others, because its expression becomes overwhelming, sometimes even violent.

So my advice is to express all of your feelings, regardless of whether you think they are acceptable, and then let them go. Buddhists understand this when they talk about nongrasping, or nonattachment to experience. By letting all emotions have their natural release, the "bad" ones are transformed to "good" ones, and in Buddhist terms, we are then liberated from suffering. When your emotions are moving and your chemicals flowing, you will experience feelings of freedom, hopefulness, joy, because you are in a healthy, "whole" state. The goal is to keep information flowing, feedback systems working, and natural balance maintained, all of which we can help to achieve by a conscious decision to enter into the bodymind's conversation."

"I believe that happiness is what we feel when our biochemicals of emotion, the neuropeptides and their receptors, are open and flowing freely throughout the psychosomatic network, integrating and coordinating our systems, organs, and cells in a smooth and rhythmic movement. Health and happiness are often mentioned in the same breath, and maybe this is why: Physiology and emotions are inseparable. I believe that happiness is our natural state, that bliss is hardwired. Only when our systems get blocked, shut down, and disarrayed do we experience the mood disorders that add up to unhappiness in the extreme."

"We found that the flow of chemicals arose from many sites in the different systems simultaneously – the immune, the nervous, the endocrine, and the gastrointestinal – and that these sites formed nodal points on a vast superhighway of internal information exchange taking place on a molecular level. We then had to consider a system with intelligence diffused throughout, rather than a one-way operation adhering strictly to the laws of cause and effect, as was previously thought when we believed that the brain ruled over all.

So, if the flow of our molecules are not directed by the brain, and the brain is just another nodal point in the network, then we must ask – Where does the intelligence, the information that runs our bodymind, come from? We know that information has an infinite capability to expand and increase, and that is beyond time and place, matter and energy. Therefore, it cannot belong to the material world we apprehend with our senses, but must belong to its own realm, one that we can experience as emotion, the mind, the spirit – an *inforealm*! This is the term I prefer, because it has a scientific ring to it, but others mean the same thing when they say field of intelligence, innate intelligence, the wisdom of the body. Still others call it God."

"The spiritual viewpoint, confirming my feeling about the religious aspect of holism, is one that sees the unity of all things, that allows us to experience our oneness with all others and with God. I can understand this on a scientific level: Yes, we have a biochemical psychosomatic network run by intelligence, an intelligence that has no bounds and that is not owned by any individual but shared among all of us in a bigger network, the macrocosm to our microcosm, the "big psychosomatic network in the sky." And in this greater network of all humanity, all life, we are each of us an individual nodal point, each an access point into a larger intelligence. It is this shared connection that gives us our most profound sense of spirituality, making us feel connected, whole.

As above, so below. To think otherwise is to suffer, to experience the stresses of separation from our source, from our true union. And what is it that flows between us all, linking and communicating, coordinating and integrating our many points? The emotions! The emotions are the connectors, flowing between individuals, moving among us as empathy, compassion, sorrow, and joy. I believe that the receptors on our cells even vibrate in response to extracorporeal peptide reaching, a phenomenon that is analogous to the strings of a resting violin responding when another violin's strings are played. We call this *emotional resonance*, and it is a scientific fact that we can feel what others feel. The oneness of all life is based on this simple reality: Our molecules of emotions are all vibrating together."

Avoiding Substance Abuse

"For the same reasons that it's best to avoid overconsuming sugar, I want to warn against the dangers of alcohol, tobacco, marijuana, cocaine, and other drugs. All of these substances have natural analogs circulating in our blood, each of which binds to its very own receptor bodywide. Alcohol, for example, binds to the GABA receptor complex, which also accommodates Valium and Librium, common prescription drugs for quelling anxiety, providing an antianxiety effect, but only in the short run. When we ingest these exogenous ligands, they compete with the natural chemicals that were meant to bind with the GABA receptors, oftentimes flooding them and thereby causing them to decrease in sensitivity and/or number. The receptors then signal a decrease in peptide secretions, as I explained in my talk to the heroin addicts in prison. All drugs can alter the natural flow of your own feel-good peptides, and so, biochemically, there is no difference between legal and illegal ones: They are potentially harmful, they can all be abused, and they can all contribute to suboptimal health in one form or another, including chronic depression.

When multiple drugs are taken, such as when a person is smoking marijuana regularly and taking antidepressants – a common situation that is often missed by the prescribing doctor – their side effects interact, and natural feedback loops of the system can collapse, leaving only a small number active.

The good news is that the physiological effects resulting from substance abuse are reversible: The heroin addict can be cured, the chronic pot smoker can kick the habit, those who think life wouldn't be worth living without antidepressants may find that they have healed sufficiently to do without them. But it can be a very slow and sometimes painful process before the receptors return to their original sensitivity and number and the corresponding peptides get back into bodywide production and flow. In recovery, what is often overlooked is that many systems – gastrointestinal, immune, and endocrine to name a few – have been affected, not just the brain. Drugs put a tremendous strain on the liver, the organ responsible for providing enzymes to metabolize the drugs and dispose of their toxic waste products. While the liver is thus overburdened and distracted, toxicity from other sources builds up, predisposing the bodymind to disease. Recovery programs, both formal ones and those we institute ourselves, need to take into account this multi-system reality by emphasizing nutritional support and exercise. Eating fresh, unprocessed foods, preferably organic vegetables, and engaging in mild exercise like walking to increase blood flow through the liver can speed the process up." – Dr. Candace Pert, PhD, *Molecules of Emotion*

You Hold the Keys to Your Healing

However, I believe, based on my research and experience, that the reality of our life is not what is happening to us physically but rather what is happening to us emotionally, of which we are not fully aware. It is the core issue, the underlying emotional story, that we are unconsciously telling ourselves in the background that determines our reactions and shows up in our conscious life experience – emotionally, mentally and physically.

Dr. Nelie Johnson's article *You Hold the Keys to Your Healing* lists the 5 Steps that support healing of major diseases:

1. Adjust your view of disease as much as possible. Think of your body "talking" to you, letting you know that it is responding to a core emotional stress or conflict, and is helping you by storing the stress energy in the physical body, so that you live well for as long as possible.

2. Be curious about your core issue (the underlying emotional story) and begin to be aware of the situations that bother or upset you the most. In other words, notice what pushes your buttons the most. Notice, too, when you go flat, get down or sad. Get to know yourself.

3. When your buttons get pushed, rather than push back with anger and irritation, ask yourself, "What is really getting to me? What is my anger? What are my deeper feelings and inner dialogue about this?" Getting upset is an opportunity to get to know yourself.

4. Begin a journal of your experiences and insights.

5. Get support to help you uncover key aspects of your emotional story. Participate in a workshop or arrange private sessions. Most of us need outside help, for we are blind to what is unconscious in us.

"We are sick because we are not aware. Awareness is the key to healing." - Anonymous

You heal the disease when you clear the cause by identifying and releasing the associated pattern of stress. When you clear stress energy, you pull the plug on disease and it has no reason for being. The body can heal itself when there is no emotional block in the way, including your own fears.

However, until you clear the stress pattern, disease continues and you need the support of medical treatment and other therapies. Be sure to work closely with your doctors and continue medical treatments for as long as they are needed.

The question to ask yourself is not only "what can this therapy or treatment do for me?" but also "what can I do for myself?" and "what do I need to know about myself and how I live my life and how I am reacting unconsciously?"

When you go after the root cause of disease or "dis-ease" you open up possibilities of deep healing. The rewards you might experience are:

- unburdening yourself of emotional distress, limiting beliefs or a physical condition

- finding freshness, energy and vitality in your life

- creating your life in the moment rather than reacting to an unconscious program and replaying the past

- experiencing greater ease, calmness and sense of well-being

Life experience can manifest as disease or illness. When you bring awareness to the emotional root cause – to the stress pattern and the associated thoughts and beliefs – you empower yourself to heal your life so you may heal physically.

Whether you have recurrent migraine headaches, fibromyalgia, a weight issue, arthritis, a cancer or an unwanted pattern in your life, it is possible to heal.

Whatever the diagnosis, you do not have to expect the worst. There are solutions. You hold the keys to your healing.

- Every disease, including every type of cancer, carries a message. The message directs you to the emotional conflict and provides you with opportunity to find another way to resolve the stress.

- You can be grateful for the message that your disease carries, for it can bring you to what you need to give special attention to.

- There is power in gratitude. It eases fear and suffering. It opens the path to Love. Love is the most powerful energy for health and healing. "

Source: *You Hold the Keys to Your Healing* by Dr. Nelie Johnson, MD
www.awarenessheals.ca

"We are sick because we are not aware. Awareness is the key to healing."

In every case of disease the brain responds instantaneously in the following ways:

- absorbs the intense shock of the experience into the subconscious and stores the memory there out of the person's full awareness. Thus the person is protected from taking on the full impact of the trauma.

Should one live the full impact consciously, one is at risk of being overwhelmed and unable to eat, sleep and pay attention to his/her surroundings. In that state the individual would not survive beyond 3 or 4 weeks.   His or her life is threatened. The primary function of the brain is to ensure survival so some action must be taken.

- manages the intense level of stress by altering the operation of a small area or focus of brain cells to run a disease or illness pattern in the body– such as migraine, fibromyalgia, MS, diabetes, cancer, infections. The severity of the disease is proportional to the degree of intensity of the stress energy.

As a result of the above actions of the brain, only a very small fraction of the brain and body are concerned with containing the stress energy. The rest of the brain and body is free to function normally to ensure the survival of the individual for as long as possible and to give time for alternative solutions to clear the stress energy to be found.

Disease is the ultimate survival strategy of the brain. It alerts the person that some aspect of his/her life, that is not part of their conscious memory, needs attention. Until the person is able to resolve the stress or conflict involved, disease contains the stress energy and supports survival.

Disease represents a band of memory for which the individual is blank – has no conscious awareness.

 Whenever you have a disease, illness, or an upset, begin to be curious about what was going on in your life before. What were you most distressed about? What were your thoughts and feelings? What were you believing?   This process of mind-body awareness can lead to release of the original stress and healing.

Source: *What are you remembering? – Healing through awareness* by Dr. Nelie Johnson, MD
www.awarenessheals.ca

GLOSSARY of Scientific Terms

Amino acids Amino acids are organic compounds that are the building blocks of proteins and the smaller peptides. Proteins are large, naturally occurring polypeptides.

Cytokine/chemokine (interleukin, lymphokine) An effort was made to systematize the nomenclature, and, as the identification of these potent biological mediators remains a subject of intense research, this process continues. For example, for a while, the name interleukin was used to emphasize the "interleukocyte" nature of the information flow, and a "lymphokine" was the hormonal secretion of a lymphocyte. However, almost as soon as these concepts were established and set forth, it became clear that such communication neither originated solely in lymphocytes nor was confined to lymphocytes. The more general term of "cytokine" emphasizes that some cytokines cause "chemotaxis." See leukocyte.

Chemotaxis The ability of cells, including bacteria and other unicellular organisms, to move toward a chemical stimulus. Because cells will move toward (chemotax) higher concentrations of the stimulus, its controlled release enables it to serve as a chemotactic meditator, recruiting cells to specific sites in the body where and when they are needed.

Endogenous Originating or produced within an organism, a tissue, or a cell. The opposite of exogenous.

GABA receptors are a class of receptors that respond to the neurotransmitter gamma-aminobutyric acid (GABA), the chief inhibitory neurotransmitter in the vertebrae central nervous system. There are two classes of GABA receptors, GABAa known as ionotropic receptors, and GABAb receptors known as metabotropic receptors.

Leukocyte A white blood cell, a generic term for the lymphocytes, monocytes, and other cells of the immune and host-defense system.

Ligand From the Latin ligare, "that which binds" (same root as religion). Any of a variety of small molecules that specifically bind to a cellular receptor and in so doing convey an informational message to the cell.

Molecule The smallest particle into which an element or a compound can be divided without changing its chemical and physical properties. A molecule is composed of several, perhaps many, atoms.

Neuron Any of the impulse-conducting cells that constitute the brain, spinal column, and nerves, consisting of a nucleated cell body with one or more dendrites and a single axon. Also called nerve cell.

Neuropeptide Any of the nearly 100 small peptide informational substances initially described as neuronal secretions. More recent observations that lymphocytes and monocytes both secrete and respond to neuropeptides has, of course, rendered this term somewhat inaccurate, and immunologists favor terms like cytokine or chemokine, but neuroscientists still commonly refer to neuropeptides.

Neurotransmitter A chemical substance, such as acetylcholine or dopamine, that transmits nerve impulses across a synapse.

Peptide Any of various natural or synthetic compounds containing two or more amino acids linked by the carboxyl group of one amino acid and the amino group of another. By definition, polypeptides are the larger peptides, usually those with in excess of 100 amino acids. But they are smaller than the proteins, which may have 200 or more amino acids as well as other attached molecules, such as sugars or lipids.

Protein A complex organic macromolecule that is composed of one or more chains of amino acids. Proteins are fundamental components of all living cells and include many substances, such as enzymes, hormones, and antibodies, that are necessary for the proper functioning of the organism.

PNI Psychoneuroimmunology. A term coined in the early eighties to emphasize and promote research that is interdisciplinary in focus and attempts to understand how mental (psychological) function affects immunological activities mediated via traditional neuronal connections. *Neuroimmunomodulation* is another variant term in which psyche is subsumed (implied) within "neuro."

Receptor A molecule, typically a protein or group of proteins, anchored in the outer cell membrane with a site accessible to the outside environment that binds with ligands such as hormones, antigens, drugs, peptides, or neurotransmitters – all those ligands been referred to as "informational substances." The receptor is the key player in the communication network of the bodymind, as it is only when the receptor is occupied by the ligand that the information encoded in the informational substances can be received. It is also at the receptor that the earliest informational processing occurs, as the actual signal the receptor transduces to the cell can be modulated by the action of other receptors and their ligands, the physiology of the cell, and even past events and memories of them.

Synapse The junction across which a nerve impulse passes from an axon terminal to a neuron, a muscle cell, or a gland cell.

YOU HOLD THE KEYS TO HEALING

"Awareness and intention are powerful factors for personal transformation and healing."

Now that the four books by Ricardo B Serrano have been published, *Meditation and Qigong Mastery, Return to Oneness with the Tao, Return to Oneness with Spirit through Pan Gu Shen Gong*, and *Keys to Healing and Self-Mastery according to the Hathors*, the important questions are, what makes these books different from other related meditation and Qigong books? What will I learn from reading these books?

These four books have the same goal: to offer readers how-to-techniques to manage stress in their daily lives and spiritually awaken when stress is cleared and released. These keys to your healing – are the *non-sectarian* how-to-techniques that have been personally practiced and developed for 30 years by the author, Ricardo B Serrano, and have been tested in clinical setting by him, his clients, and other Taoist, Buddhist and Yoga meditation and Qigong practitioners of every *pantheistic* – All is God – tradition for centuries for healing and personal transformation.

The first book *Meditation and Qigong Mastery* elaborates on the meditation and Qigong principles that masters use to activate and develop their lightbodies, also called EMF (electromagnetic fields), Wei Qi or merkaba, which is the missing mastery principle not discussed by eastern authors in their meditation and Qigong books. Omkabah heart lightbody activation and Maitreya (Shiva) Shen Gong are introduced. Quotations on inner mastery by meditation masters are included to guide the readers toward the path of inner mastery. Powerful mantras are also included to unite the meditation practitioners to the spiritual divine energy of the ancient lineage of the Siddha and Buddhist Masters. Lastly, the merkaba energy ball of light with holographic sound healing is taught for healing and spiritual awakening.

The second book *Return to Oneness with the Tao* elaborates on the Taoist meditation and Qigong inner alchemy techniques such as lower dantien breathing, Microcosmic Orbit Qigong, primordial wuji Qigong, meditation on twin hearts, and Tibetan Shamanic Qigong to cultivate the Three Treasures Jing, Qi and Shen. An important addition to this book is the understanding of a most important principle – awareness and intention are powerful factors for personal transformation and healing. When we are aware of what is – the emotional root cause of disease that is blocking the flow of Qi – we can intentionally release it through meditation and Qigong to effect a process of change for personal transformation and healing.

"God Consciousness is the reality of everything." – Shiva Sutra 1.1

The third book *Return to Oneness with Spirit through Pan Gu Shen Gong* elaborates on the use of Pan Gu Shen Gong together with the EFT Qi-healer's Method to effectively clear and release the emotional debris held in the body, cultivate the Three Treasures Jing, Qi and Shen, and strengthen one's self-awareness through an integrated combination of Toltec wisdom, Qigong, Qi-healing, emotional freedom technique therapy, ear acupuncture, and Chinese tonic herbs. We are sick because we are not aware. Awareness is the key to healing.

The goal of this fourth book *Keys to Healing and Self-Mastery according to the Hathors,* a supplementary book to *Holographic Sound Healing* taught at the *Meditation and Qigong Mastery book,* and the *Omkabah Heart Lightbody Activation video,* is to build the *Ka* and offer readers an effective Hathor's emotional mastery technique to manage emotional stress, the main cause of disease, in their daily lives and spiritually awaken when emotional stress is cleared, released and stabilized. Basically, the emotional mastery technique – Ka (Merkaba) Meditation – is simply connecting your awareness (attention) to the pranic tube – chong mai (neutral core) in the center of the body according to Chinese Medical Qigong Therapy – and intentionally allowing the prana or Qi from the Sun above and Earth below to flow in the pranic tube together with *opening the heart to unconditional love* and *activating the Ka or Merkaba*. Doing this practice will provide a fast, safe way to stabilize your chaotic emotions such anger or fear. Holographic Sound Healing with the Four Sacred Elements is integrated with Ka (Merkaba) Meditation to complement Holographic Lightbody activation, and build the *Sahhu* or *immortal golden lightbody*. Dr. Johanna Budwig's *Diet for Cancer and Chronic Diseases* and *Sun gazing* are included as adjunct keys to healing.

In summary, the four books *Meditation and Qigong Mastery, Return to Oneness with the Tao, Return to Oneness with Spirit* and *Keys to Healing and Self-Mastery according to the Hathors* form a *four-sided basic pyramid foundation, so to speak,* of dietary and energy-based psychoneuroimmunolgy or neuroimmunomodulation strategies to effectively heal substance abuse and chronic diseases mainly caused by emotional stress, high fat diet that is high in *trans-fatty acids and low in Essential Fatty Acids,* and *unhealthy* lifestyle (*drinking, smoking, binge eating, not exercising, shiftwork*, etc.). These strategies bring the physical, mental, emotional, and spiritual aspects of a person into homeostasis, and at the same time spiritually awaken a person in the process of being in the flow because the individual being is one with universal being.

The reality of this whole universe is God consciousness. It is filled with God consciousness.

This world is nothing but the blissful energy of the all-pervading consciousness of God. God and the individual are one, to realize this is the essence and goal of meditation and Qigong.

Whatever the diagnosis of your disease, you do not have to expect the worst. For every problem, there are solutions. You hold the keys to healing.

For those people who are interested to learn the keys to healing and naturally heal and empower themselves, more information on these books and videos are covered at www.keystohealing.ca, and www.qigongmastery.ca. The books *Meditation and Qigong Mastery, Return to Oneness with the Tao,* and *Return to Oneness with Spirit through Pan Gu Shen Gong* together *Keys to Healing and Self-Mastery according to the Hathors* can be ordered at amazon.com, createspace.com, bookstores and online retailers.

Quotations on Vibrational Medicine

According to the late *Dr. Richard Gerber*, "Vibrational medicine is a diagnostic and healing approach to illness using energy in various forms and frequencies. As a therapy, vibrational medicine is the application of different types of energy for healing, including approaches as traditional as X-ray and radiation therapy for cancer, the use of electrical nerve stimulation for treating pain, and electromagnetic field stimulators for accelerating the healing of fractured bones. Even full spectrum light is used for treating seasonal affective disorders or the 'winter blues'. However, vibrational medicine also covers the more subtle forms of treatment such as acupuncture, homeopathy, flower essences, therapeutic touch, and that sort of genre. The latter involve using subtle life-force medicine, but they are energetic therapies nonetheless. This is the spectrum from the more traditional to a range of therapies that stress treatment of the whole person, sometimes referred to as 'complementary' medicine.

I think modern medicine is wonderful. We have very effective treatments for a variety of illnesses from which people died earlier in this century. But we are seeing the limitations of technological medicine in many ways: the high cost of medicine today limits people's access to health care; in industrialized nations, chronic degenerative diseases such as arthritis, diabetes, cancer and heart disease are not curable, but are only palliated by our treatments. And in many cases the side effects of some of our treatments are worse than the disease.

The potential of non-invasive energy medicine to benefit people at a much lower cost is phenomenal. However, because the drug industry is so entrenched within the US medical system, when research money is granted, it is very much biased toward the pharmacologic approach. Molecular biology is the new buzzword, and systems that exist outside of that are not getting the research funds they deserve.

Vibrational medicine has the potential to scan the body not only for illness states, but also for a disposition toward illness, that is, a pre-physical energetic disturbance that will lead to illness. There are a variety of diagnostic systems that are evolving. One of these involves assessing the acupuncture meridian system. If we can detect disturbances in the etheric body before physical disease develops, then we have the basis for a whole new level of preventive medicine, which we have never really seen before.

Vibrational medicine is the first scientific approach I've seen that is able to integrate science and spirituality, something which has unfortunately been left out of the medical model. It's only by viewing the body as a multi-dimensional energy system that we begin to approach how the soul manifests through molecular biology, if you will. Ultimately, that comes down to the whole issue of reincarnation and karma. It's a difficult issue to grasp, especially for the larger medical community. They still have problems buying into homeopathy, let alone reincarnation. I think it is an area we need to begin to explore. There are various people doing past life regression work who are beginning to envision the soul's progress through life, and illness as an expression of obstacles the soul is trying to overcome in the whole process of learning. How karma fits into this is a very individualized thing.

The vibrational practitioners influence the individual's consciousness, helping them gain insight into the factors predisposing toward the creation of their illness, or why the illness crystallized at this time in their life. As to what are the effects of past life carry-overs, I don't have a simple answer, and it's something I'm still grappling with.

What I have discovered is that the most powerful healing force in the universe is love, unconditional love. When you work from that level you begin to open up whole vistas of discovery in self-exploration and spiritual transformation. You begin a new level of healing, not just fixing the body, but helping the individual to grow to a whole new understanding of their life and their awareness as an evolving spiritual being.

I think we need to work together on a spiritual level if we are going to create the kind of healing research center that I have envisioned and that many others have dreamed of. In order for us to create a healing center of lasting value and benefit to the planet, the scientists and the workers who come together will need to have a higher perspective of spiritual unification. We have to be aligned with the higher spiritual sense and purpose in order for us to manifest this goal. If we are, then I think we can really change the entire medical system. One of the secondary agendas of the healing research center is to heal not just people, but the planet."

Richard Gerber, MD, is the author of the 1988 book, *Vibrational Medicine: New Choices for Healing Ourselves*, a publication that has been reviewed as 'landmark' and 'encyclopedic', and in many ways bridges the gap between science and esoteric healing. Vibrational Medicine cites hundreds of scientific studies that support the energy model of health and healing and presents the theoretical foundation for such therapies as homeopathy and acupuncture.

Quotations on Holograms and Spiritual Healing

Hologram is an energy interference pattern.
Within this pattern, every piece contains the whole.

The holographic model sets a precedent for new ways of understanding Einsteinian medicine and provides a totally new way of looking at the universe. Utilizing the holographic model, it is possible to arrive at conclusions one might not come upon by utilizing simple deductive reasoning and logic.

Etheric matter is referred to in the Eastern esoteric literature as "subtle matter," or matter which is less dense than physical, i.e., of a higher frequency nature. The etheric body appears to be a subtle counterpart of the physical body, possibly somewhat like the phantom leaf. Our etheric body is an energy interference pattern with the characteristics of a hologram. It is likely that there are subtle counterparts to the physical universe made up of matter of higher frequencies. If the energy interference pattern of a single etheric body acts as a hologram, might not the entire universal energy interference pattern represent a vast cosmic hologram? If this is true, then by virtue of the holographic principle whereby every piece contains the whole, there are profound implications for information being stored within the seemingly empty space around us! The fact that limitless amounts of information might be enfolded into the structure of the universe is an idea gaining more and more attention from theorists such as Nobel prize-winning physicist David Bohm. Bohm has presented convincing scientific arguments for what he calls the "implicate order" of the holographic universe. In such a universe, higher levels of order and information may be holographically enfolded in the fabric of space and matter/energy.

If indeed there exists a cosmic hologram, then every piece of the universe contains information concerning the makeup of the entire cosmos. Unlike a static hologram, the cosmic hologram is a dynamically moving system that changes from microsecond to microsecond. *Because what happens in just a small fragment of the holographic energy interference pattern affects the entire structure simultaneously, there is a tremendous connectivity relationship between all parts of the holographic universe.* If one were to view God as "all there is," then, through the holographic interconnectivity of space, God could simultaneously be in contact with all creations. The ultimate question, of course, is how does one tap into this information about the cosmos which is enfolded into the structure of space within and around us? How do we decode the cosmic hologram?

By decoding a small piece of the universal hologram, one may unfold information about the whole universe stored within the matrix. The selective focusing of consciousness via psychic attunement (Merkaba) may hold the potential for such decoding of the universal hologram.

The Einsteinian viewpoint of vibrational medicine sees the human being as a multidimensional organism made up of physical/cellular systems in dynamic interplay with complex regulatory energetic fields. Vibrational medicine attempts to heal illness by manipulating these subtle-energy fields via directing energy into the body instead of manipulating the cells and organs through drugs or surgery.

The recognition that all matter is energy forms the foundation for understanding how human beings can be considered dynamic energetic systems. Through his famous equation, $E = mc^2$, Albert Einstein proved to scientists that energy and matter are dual expressions of the same universal substance. That universal substance is a primal energy or vibration of which we are all composed. Therefore, attempting to heal the body through the manipulation of this basic vibrational or energetic level of substance can be thought of as vibrational medicine. Although the Einsteinian viewpoint has slowly found acceptance and application in the minds of physicists, Einstein's profound insights have yet to be incorporated into the way doctors look at human beings and illness.

Vibrational medicine seeks to reunite the personality with the Higher Self in a more meaningful, connected way. Vibrational modalities help to strengthen the energetic connections between the personality and the soul itself, by rebalancing the body / mind / spirit complex as a whole. Not all vibrational healing tools work at the higher energetic levels, but it is the intent and goal of the vibrational healer / physician to seek and assist this alignment within his or her patients.

Spiritual healing (holographic healing) attempts to work at the level of the higher subtle bodies and chakras to affect a healing from the most primary level of disease origins. *The spiritual healer (holographic healer) works as a power source of multiple-frequency outputs to allow energy shifts at several levels simultaneously.* It is theorized that there may be a transient energy link between the chakras of the healer and the patient. This chakra-to-chakra link may allow for a direct resonant transfer of multiple subtle frequencies, which can shift the multidimensional energy structure of the patient back toward a perfect balance of mind, body, and spirit. *While most magnetic healers work strictly at the level of the body, spiritual healers (holographic healers) usually work with the many levels of mind and spirit as well.* The nature of this higher dimensional energy is that it transcends all limitations of space and time by virtue of the fact that levels from the etheric and higher energies are in the domain of negative space / time. As such, the energies working at these levels move in a dimension which is outside of the usual references of ordinary (or positive) space / time to which the conscious mind is limited in its perception. However, the frequencies at which spiritual healing takes place often extend to the same levels at which the Higher Self exists and operates.

"Spiritual healing" (holographic healing) works not only at the physical and etheric levels, but also helps to rebalance the astral, mental, and higher energetic levels of dysfunction as well. In addition, spiritual healing may be performed either in the presence of the patient or at great distances which may separate the patient and healer.

*If we are beings of energy, then it follows
that we can be affected by energy.*

Vibrational healing modalities are effective because of their ability to impact upon the subtle unseen hierarchical levels of human physiology, which include the physical and etheric bodies, the acupuncture meridians, the chakras and nadis, and the astral, mental, causal, and higher spiritual bodies. Having described the function and integration of these many levels of energetic and spiritual physiology, *we must now ask how all of this information fits in with our divine purpose upon the planet Earth.* An understanding of the higher levels of subtle anatomy and their influence upon our daily lives and health will help us to comprehend how we are all intimately linked with the continually evolving divine energies of the soul.

Our physical and higher bodies are specialized vehicles which allow the expression of the soul's consciousness upon the dense Earth plane. The consciousness of each soul is actually a particularization of that greater spiritual consciousness which we refer to as God. Various spiritual philosophies look to the time of our universe's creation as the period when God created all souls simultaneously. Mixing cosmic evolution with theology, one might view the Big Bang as more than just the creation of primordial interstellar hydrogen and light. It was also the time at which the Creator gave birth to the billions of human souls that would inhabit the new universe through an explosive particularization of the divine conscious energies. It is said that God created human beings in the divine image. As each soul was created in that first moment, God separated into smaller beings of light which were energetic representations of the original vast beingness. *Through the conscious evolution of these lesser gods and the holographic connectivity of the universe, God could enrich and develop the tremendous potential for diversity and self-knowledge inherent in supreme consciousness.* These primal beings of light, or souls, developed ways of manifesting the ethereal energies of their consciousness through denser forms of expression. The denser forms, called the physical bodies, would allow them to experience through their senses the wonders and beauties of the evolving planets. Also, it would allow them to experiment with the expression of their emotional nature through interactions and relationships between themselves, their environment, and the other sentient life forms manifesting upon the planets on which they chose to incarnate.

Because no entity could develop itself in all possible ways through the course of a single life span of these dense vehicles of expression, a continuous cycle of regeneration and rebirth, known as reincarnation, was created. During each lifetime, the incarnating soul is able to partake of many diverse experiences which allow it to explore the wonders, joys, and sorrows of human existence. Through hit or miss, and reward or punishment, the consciousness of the soul, projected through earthly bodies, can learn and experience planetary life through every conceivable variation of the human form. Via the reincarnation cycle, each soul comes to know the splendor and achievements, as well as the difficulties and sadnesses, of each of the existing races and colors of peoples. All souls come to experience life as the pinnacle of high society as well as the simplicity and daily toil of the farms and fields. All conscious entities find out how life differs between being male and female in the different societies. Through each of these varied experiences, the soul comes to know itself and to better understand its own emotional, physical, and spiritual nature, as well as the many different expressions that physical human life allows. *Perhaps most importantly in its earthly sojourns, the soul comes to appreciate and experience the nature of love in its many different forms, and develops a greater compassion and caring for all of God's creations.*

Personal and spiritual transformation are dependent upon the opening of the heart chakra. As our heart centers open wider and we begin to feel greater compassion and empathy for all living things, we move closer to expressing the divine unconditional love of the Christ Consciousness, which is the supreme facet of spiritual awakening towards which we are all gradually evolving.

Of the chakra blockages that are known to occur, dysfunction in the heart chakra can be the most devastating. *The heart chakra is the central energy center in the chakra / nadi system.* It is an integral link between the three higher and the three lower chakras. In another sense, it is also the center of human existence, because it is the major chakra from which we are able to express love. *The expression of love is perhaps one of the most important lessons that humans have incarnated upon the physical plane to learn. Without love, existence can be dry and meaningless. It is necessary that we learn to love not only those around us but also ourselves.*

All souls are spiritual beings of light which remain energetically connected to the Creator and the Creator's universe through a holographic connectivity relationship. All souls have evolved as unique but diverse manifestations of the single divine principle (also known as the Law of One). As the souls become enriched through their experiences, so too does the Creator come to grow and evolve in a greater knowing of self in infinite expression. In spite of this unity with God and the universe, the souls temporary lose the memory of their spiritual origins after incarnating into dense physical bodies. *In reality, the higher spiritual bodies of the souls maintain a cosmic awareness and connection to the God-force. Only the projected fragment of the soul's total consciousness which inhabits the dense physical form loses the memory of its origins.*

The earthly personalities forget that they are manifestations of the one supreme intelligence, as the perceptual mechanisms of their brains and bodies create a physical sense of separation from each other as well as from their Creator. Partly because of this sense of separation from God, human beings have created religion and its rituals in an attempt to reunite themselves with the creative forces of nature and the physical universe which seemed outside of themselves. Human beings forget that the kingdom of God is already within each of us. Jesus (Lord Sananda) incarnated to teach and remind us of this simple forgotten truth.

The reincarnational cycle has built-in safeguards that prevent the perpetuation of wrong thinking and negative actions toward fellow journeyers upon the soul quest of self-discovery and enlightenment. This system of energy credits and debits, based on positive and negative deeds and actions, has been referred to as the Law of Karma. The subtle nature of higher dimensional anatomy and its controlling influence upon the creation and physiological maintenance of the physical body, allows the negative energies of past-life misdeeds to be carried over to future lifetimes by causing subtle abnormalities in the human physical and emotional structure.

By working through physical handicaps and illnesses, individuals are able to "burn away the karma" of their negative deeds and redeem their souls for the evils, torments, and suffering that they may have caused others in previous lives.

Karmic illness is worth mentioning because it is an area of disease upon which vibrational medicine is able to have certain impacts, at least in creating an awareness of the reasons behind some diseases and handicaps. Again, this returns us to the concept of self-responsibility in accepting the consequences of our actions, whether they originate from this life or a past one. Few would dream that the negative emotions and malicious deeds of their previous lives would come back to haunt them in their present lives as some form of illness. But it is possible, nonetheless.

The most important things that Jesus (Lord Sananda) taught – learning to love ourselves and others, to forgive, and to pray and give thanks to the Creator – are just as important today as they were 2000 years ago. We have seen how distortions of our emotional nature, and blockage of our ability to love and forgive, can cause disturbance and imbalance of our chakras and subtle-energy anatomy. When one combines weakness of the body's energetic physiology from emotional, mental, and subtle imbalances, with infectious or toxic environmental factors, illness is often the result. Through the sophisticated New Age technologies which spiritual scientists are using to document the existence of our subtle anatomic framework, we are finally beginning to understand the true spiritual significance of what Jesus (Lord Sananda) and many others have taught throughout the centuries since the time of Lemuria and Atlantis. *The discoveries that we are making today are, in fact, reincarnational expressions of older spiritual knowledge which originated in these ancient yet advanced civilizations.*

The basic principles of holistic and natural healing, as well as vibrational medicine, are actually thousands of centuries old, dating back to the times of Atlantis and Lemuria. Through the continuous cycle of regeneration and rebirth, these ideas have surfaced once again to produce methods of spiritual healing (such as holographic healing) that may help to alleviate much of the disease that humanity seems to have inflicted upon itself. It is only because of a gradual shift in consciousness within the new guard of the medical and scientific community that the intellectual and spiritual environment has ripened to the point that these powerful healing modalities may again surface to see the light of day.

"The expression of love is perhaps one of the most important lessons that humans have incarnated upon the physical plane to learn. Without love, existence can be dry and meaningless. It is necessary that we learn to love not only those around us but also ourselves. "

- Excerpts from Vibrational Medicine by Dr. Richard Gerber, 1988.

HOLOGRAPHIC HEALING WITH SOUND

According to Dr. Richard Gerber's Vibrational Medicine book, "Sound therapy is one of the prototypical vibrational healing modalities. Sound produces measurable vibratory feelings throughout the body, depending upon the frequency and amplitude of the sound used. There have been a wide variety of sound healing developments over the last ten to twenty years. Certain sounds most likely have a healing influence upon the body because they influence the geometric patterns and organization of cells and living systems. "

As a Traditional Chinese medical (TCM) practitioner, the following excerpt from the Vibrational Medicine book talks about the use of sound healing in Chinese medicine, "The concept of a specific frequency of sound associated with each part of the seven chakras is not new. Various East Indian yoga teachings ascribe particular notes of music to each of the seven chakras. Another ancient system associating musical notes with subtle-energy systems of the body is the five Element Theory of acupuncture and Chinese medicine. The Chinese model views Earth and the human body in terms of the five elements of creation, which are fire, earth, metal, water, and wood. Each of the five elements is associated with particular acupuncture meridians and organ systems that energetically interact within the body according to the Law of the Five Elements and its cycles of energy flow. In addition to each element being linked to a particular organ system, it also has a particular musical note associated with it. The five musical notes of the Five Element System comprise of a pentatonic scale that has been used in China as a basis of musical composition and improvisation. Melodies with emphasis on particular elemental notes have been developed in China to stimulate healing of the various organ systems of the body.

Intricate musical tone studies done by the Shanghai Chinese Traditional Orchestra resulted in a series of six tapes, collectively known as Yi Ching Music for health. Yi Ching music is actually a healing music based on the Five Element Theory of Chinese medicine. These are particular songs or musical compositions associated with each of the five elements. To use the healing compositions for a particular illness, one would analyze the illness in terms of classical Chinese medicine. For instance, in Five Element Theory, the liver meridian and organ are associated with the element wood. To assist in healing an individual who has a liver disease, such as hepatitis, you would utilize "Wood Music" to help balance the element wood in the body. The wood music may stimulate balanced flow of energy in the liver meridians that feed nutritional Qi (energy) to the liver organ.

Healing with musical compositions based on the energy systems of ancient Chinese medicine is one of the many varied approaches to healing with sound. It is a unique example of ancient healing principles merging with new vibrational concepts to provide yet another sound healing system. Perhaps future research will verify the particular healing benefits of each sonic healing technology, alone, or in combination with other vibrational healing modalities."

Holographic Sound Healing technology – healing the body through the chakras with sound – as I have learned and experienced it is a powerful ancient/new sound healing system which should be utilized as an important part of vibrational healing modalities as used in my TCM clinical practice.

When you do sound healing, the sound resonates from you and moves energy to remove unwanted blocks or beliefs, like a thread between you and the other person. Sound stirs energy at deep levels, releasing all emotions and increasing the flow of intention. Cells have vibrational memories and just have to be reminded to release and balance themselves. – Renee Brodie, The Healing Tones of Crystal Bowls

"What made me interested in healing with sound? Why does Healing with Sound work?" *you might have asked.*

Whenever I am listening to my CDs such as Angel Love and Elevation 2 during my meditation sessions and also whenever I am playing my piano, singing my kareoke and especially tuning my crystal bowl during holographic sound healing that I always noticed the supportive effect of music and sound to the strength, power and expansion of my consciousness and light body Merkaba especially its soothing effect to my feeling or emotional nature.

There has to be a reason or an explanation to why sound has this effect to my emotional body which was answered by Barbara Marciniak's Bringers of Dawn - Teachings from the Pleiadians book, *"Emotion, because it brings feeling and connects you to feeling, allows you to recognize different states of consciousness. The logical mind does not allow you to recognize states of consciousness because it holds onto its own identity. It is locked into the boundary of ego and does not want to recognize other areas. Feeling, however, always acknowledges other areas because feeling discerns the difference. You can read the signs and the definitions by the energy that you call feeling. It is, in actuality, a vibration.* **Sound brings about states of emotional feeling.** *When you create harmonics of sound, it reminds your body of something. It reminds your body of Light, of deep Cosmic love and other worlds. Your body comes into joy and sometimes overwhelmingly into sadness. It seeks and accesses a frequency that it has been longing for, of which the sound has reminded it. As you allow your sound to play your body, you discover a frequency that you have sought. This frequency is connected to the evolution of the helixes within your body. Sound is a vehicle or conduit to connect you to the* **higher chakras outside your body** *because you do not have a way of accessing them logically.* **You must access all frequencies and chakra centers by feelings,** *and* **sound will connect you with feeling,** *which will allow you to understand the information.*

If sound could be pictured, some of you would become entranced with watching it. There are realities where sound does picture itself. You feel the movement and language of sounds when you wave your body or move your hands. You experience the richness of this form of communication and how multi-dimensional all things are by feeling sound express itself. It has its own language, and it has a form."

As a registered acupuncturist of BC, I have always been searching for alternative healing technologies I could integrate with my Traditional Chinese medical modalities. Sound healing is definitely a very powerful healing modality as discovered by a fellow French acupuncturist and musician, Fabien Maman. Dr. Carolyn Shreeve's Journal of Alternative & Complementary Medicine article called "How Far is Sound & Colour Therapy Medicine of the Future?" where she quoted, *"Maman also **teaches his patients to sing the curative note,** rather like a chant or a mantra. He has synthesized aspects of his knowledge of sound with the use of movement, meditation and colour into a complete healing system. Movement (he uses Qi Gong) regenerates the life force in the meridians. This he believes links us to cosmic energy and when practiced with our fundamental sound, starts up vibrations within the individual's morphogenetic field.*

*It may well be true, as Fabien Maman claims, that colour links us to the energy of the planets, that it can be used to "clarify the astral plane," and that **sound,** because it surrounds vibrating particles and increases their spin, facilitates their expansion and widens our field of consciousness. **Maman's research with cancer and sound may turn out to be one of the most significant and exciting discoveries of this century.***

*Maman's particular contribution has been to discover that certain specific sound frequencies transmitted to acupuncture points by **Tuning Forks are as effective as needles** in treating patients. His interest was further stimulated by his meeting with the French physicist and musician, Joel Sternheimer. Sternheimer has discovered that elementary particles vibrate at frequencies in accordance with musical laws; he views the material world as an aspect of music. Since then, Maman and Sternheimer have worked together, successfully investigating the harmonic and melodic equivalents of living matter. They claimed they have found that **all meridian lines, acupuncture points, tissues and organs have their own individual "musical note".** Moreover, they are in constant state of flux, affected by such factors as the seasons, time of day and night and so on, and therefore have constantly changing sound equivalents.*

*A particular achievement of the pair has been the transposition of the characteristic vibratory resonance of certain key molecules into their lower frequency musical equivalents. The effect of this is to slow down the vibrational rate of the molecules concerned. Maman contends that this process has enormously **important therapeutic implications** in that it can be used both to stimulate healthy human cells and to harmonise and heal sick ones. He also emphasises the adverse effects of environmental noise, which should be significantly reduced if the human organism is to reach its potential of vitality and well-being. In his clinical research, with the biologist Helene Grimaud and others, he discovered that blood cells, subjected to a chromatic scale of sound frequencies, became colored and altered their shape according to the particular frequency employed. The note A (440 hertz) changed them to Pink, C made them longer, E made them round, and D produced considerable colour variety.*

When Cancer Cells were subjected likewise to a chromatic scale, their intracellular components started to lose definition as the scale ascended, and generally disintegrated between A (440 hertz) and B. Individual cells have "personal" qualities related to the overall condition of the person from whom they are taken. This partly accounts for the fact that when sound is used therapeutically, cure is achieved in some cases and not in others. Maman determines the level at which energy is depleted - physical, etheric, astral, mental, psychic or spiritual - and decides which sound frequency to use through pulse examination, the use of instinct and by listening to the patient's voice. Just as the correct note is therapeutic, so inappropriate ones can cause damage. Sounds are therefore highly specific in each case, and are applied through tuning forks to acupuncture points or chakras (energy centers), or by means of headphones."

We hear and ingest sounds with more than the auditory mechanism of our ears. The whole body responds to sound and consumes it, whether we consciously hear the sound or not. Consider how the mind tunes out the ticking of a clock or the humming of a refrigerator. But even though the conscious mind can filter out the sound, the body cannot. The human body vibrates too. Each beat of the heart shakes the entire body, and the body responds to this vibration. Its response may be measured by a miniature seismograph.

– Steven Halpern with Louis Savary, Sound Health - The Music and Sound that Makes Us Whole

"What is the basis of sound healing? What is resonance? What does it do? How does resonance affect one? What causes the resonance with Crystal Bowls? Does this affect one's health, one's balance of energies, one's level of energy?" you might have asked.

According to Jonathan Goldman's Healing Sounds book, *"**Resonance** is the basis of every sound therapy that I have examined. As you may recall, **resonance** is the basic vibratory rate of an object. Everything in the universe is in a state of vibration. This includes the human body. Every organ, bone, tissue and other part of the body has a healthy resonant frequency. When that frequency alters, that part of the body vibrates out of harmony and this is what is termed dis-ease. If it were possible to determine the correct resonant frequency for a healthy organ and then project it into that part which is dis-eased, the organ should return to its normal frequency and a healing should occur.*

*When an organ or another part of the body is in a state of health, it will be creating a natural resonant frequency that is harmonious with the rest of the body. However, when dis-ease sets in, a different sound pattern is established in that part of the body which is not vibrating in harmony. Therefore, it is possible, through use of externally created sound that is projected into the dis-eased area, to reintroduce the correct harmonic pattern .. and effect a curative reaction. Through the **principle of resonance**, sound can be used to change disharmonious frequencies of the body back to their normal, healthful vibrations.*

*The different rhythms of the body may also be changed through sound. This is known as **"entrainment"** and involves the ability of the more powerful rhythmic vibrations of one object to change the less powerful rhythmic vibrations of another object and cause them to synchronize their rhythms with the first object. Through sound it is possible to change the rhythms of our brain waves, as well as our heartbeat and respiration.*

*It has been verified recently that sound can be used to affect and change our brain waves. These principles of using **resonance and entrainment** are the fundamental concepts behind the use of sound to heal and transform. They are found in every practice that uses sound, regardless of tradition, belief system or culture. ... Examination of these practices, from the Hindu use of mantras to shamanic use of chanting and drumming, reveals a commonality in these principles of resonance and entrainment as the basis of sonic transformation and healing."*

According to John Beauliu's Music and Sound in the Healing Arts: An Energy Approach book, *"**Resonance** occurs when the vibrations of one object reach out and set off vibrations in another object. The word **"resonance"** comes from the Latin verb **resonare**, meaning **"to return to sound"**. If the two objects have closely similar frequencies and one is vibrated, the other object will also sound, e.g. if you have two tuning forks of the same pitch and you strike one, the other will also make sound. This is called **"sympathetic resonance"**.*

***Resonance** is the (pitch) intonation of a certain note which resonates, find its level in unison with your pitch or frequency, causing a harmony to take place. It is very healing and is composed of like frequencies meeting each other, being agreeable if you will. You may feel you resonate with someone, as opposed to dissonance (disagreeable) and that is simply the reverse. To resonate with, is to be in harmony with that person, or note or object, and if you are, then your notes are balanced, not jarring in any way, peaceful, full of strength and also joyfulness.*

*The intervals of the tuning forks create a sympathetic resonance with the quality of **Sacred Sound** deep within us. The archetype begins to align our thoughts and physical body around its vibration, e.g. when the forks are tapped, it is quite common to observe the head and body move and adjust to the proportions of the sound. If we look at our bodies as actual manifestations of the pattern of the **Sacred Sound**, we can begin to understand how the sound of the tuning forks can be used for healing".*

According to Olivia Dewhurst-Maddock's The Book of Sound Therapy book, *"The acoustic principle of **resonance** applies not only to musical instruments, but also to the human body. As the sound waves enter the body, sympathetic vibrations occur in its living cells, which help to restore and reinforce healthy organization. **The high water content of the body's tissues helps to conduct sound, and the overall effect is likened to a deep massage at the atomic and molecular level.***

The human being is therefore likened to a very complex, unique, and finely-tuned musical instrument. Every atom, molecule, cell, tissue, and organ of the body continually broadcast the frequencies of physical, emotional, mental, and spiritual life. The human voice is an indicator of its body's health on all these levels of existence. It establishes a relationship between the individual and the wondrous network of vibrations that is the cosmos."

According to Deborah Van Dyke's The Soul Garden book, *"The knowledge of sound carries with it great power. It allows one to travel without moving. In creation myths all over the world, sound is recognized as the source of all visible and invisible things. **Sound is vibration and vibration is music in a three-dimensional form**. When sand is placed on a sheet of glass and the sheet is stroked with the bow of a violin, the sand instantly arranges itself into beautiful geometric shapes, like a mandala.*

*Sound creates and sound arranges. The harmonics created by the playing of singing bowls have an amazing therapeutic effect on people. When you strike a singing bowl, you can feel that the air surrounding the bowl also vibrates. The powerful vibrations spread quickly through the body which consists of approximately 90% water after all, and this results in a very delicate internal massage of all the cells. The human body is a living entity of vibrations and wavelengths. **A healthy organ is well tuned, meaning that it vibrates only at its own frequency, while the frequency of a sick organ is disturbed.** Singing bowls recreate the original harmonic frequency, and stimulate the body to rediscover its own harmonic frequency, by making it vibrate to the frequency of the bowl so that when it is synchronized, it can vibrate independently. Stimulated and taken up by the power vibrations of the singing bowl, the body is able to tune into its own undisturbed frequency."*

"What then is the aim of sound in healing?"

*According to Renee Brodie, "This is the aim of sound, for you to **resonate** with a piece of music, or the tone you sound yourself, or a particular Bowl so that its sound **"waves"** through you, touches where it is needed, and balances. Then you are healed, your auric field is **"in flow"** and you will radiate perfect health."*

"Sound is an energy form generated by a vibrating body. Depending on its frequency, the human body will react to and perceive this energy in different ways. If the pitch is below the audible level and the amplitude is high, we may feel it although we do not hear it. If it is within the audible range, we will hear it and classify it according to our knowledge of sound. If the pitch is ultrasonic – above the audible range – we will not hear it but may experience unpleasant bodily reactions to what is known as White Sound."

The Thymus, Immune System and Sound Healing

"The immune system which includes the thymus gland, lymph nodes, bone marrow, spleen, tonsils, adenoids, appendix, Peyer's Patches are all connected, and all are affected by color and sound. Care then is needed daily to nourish ourselves with appropriate colors for us – and to be very aware that all sounds affect the Thymus gland and therefore, that Chakra."

Renee Brodie, The Healing Tones of Crystal Bowls

"What is the Thymus gland? What is its function? its connection to the Immune System?" *you might have asked.*

The Thymus gland, at the forward base of the neck, plays a key role in the immunological defense system, stimulating production of white blood cells that fight disease and infection. The thymus gland is fairly large at birth and continues to grow until adolescence, when it begins to shrink. By middle age the thymus is much smaller, but it is still an important factor in the immune system. During the first few weeks of life, T-lymphocytes created in the thymus migrate to the blood stream and colonize lymph nodes through the body. These later begin to manufacture powerful antibodies vital for immunity.

According to Dr. John Diamond's Your Body Doesn't Lie book, *"In the second century, Galen gave the name Thymus to the pinkish-grey two-lobed organ in the chest because, it is said, it reminded him of a bunch of thyme. But the thyme plant itself was so-named because it was burned as incense to the gods. Thymus (Greek) then was a rising up of smoke, a burning of incense, a sacrificing up to the gods - all taking place in the chest, the inner altar. It was aspiration, songs of praise, spirit, and the putting out of love. It was the breath-soul, on which depended a man's energy and courage. So the Thymus is the Seat of Life Energy.*

Modern medical science has not always understood the function of the thymus gland... Now, medicine recognizes the thymus gland is closely related to the immune system, stress, and general well-being.

Earlier this century it was thought the Thymus gland had no function beyond puberty. It simply atrophied... a delusion fostered by finding during autopsy that the gland was quite small. It is now known that in response to acute stress such as infection, it can shrivel to half the size within 24 hours. Earlier, doctors thought that after puberty the Thymus had no useful function, and in many young children it was excised! This destroyed a vital part of their Immune System, allowing them to become susceptible to infections and chronic disease. Later in the 1950s and after research it became clear that children naturally have large thymus glands and some dying from serious illness or great physical stress had died before the gland had time to shrink.

After puberty it diminishes in size because it is no longer concerned with growth. Any further shrinkage is due to stress and other factors. The dramatic shrinkage of the thymus gland in a person undergoing stress is not fully understood. Within a day of severe injury or sudden illness, millions of lymphocytes are destroyed and the thymus shrinks to half its size. This part of the general reaction to stress described by Dr. Hans Seyle. We also know that that the thymus continues to secrete hormones and T cells until late in life. This role is known as immunological surveillance so another function has been added to the so-called "inactive" thymus gland.

It is only recently that the immunological functions of this gland have been understood. It has the role of Master Controller that directs life-giving and healing energies of the body, and is strongly influenced by an individual's physical environment, social relationships, food and posture."

"How are we then able to heal the overstressed Thymus gland?"

According to Renee Brodie, *"Our immune system functions more effectively when we are happy and creative, and affects every cell in our body when its energy flow is harmonious. When we feel out-of-sorts, unwell, the cells of the immune system do not "ring true", and this will affect every part of us. We see now how important the Thymus chakra is to our well-being.*

We know that through the newly-awakened Thymus chakra, we can absolutely work towards balancing this energy center and therefore the immune system, until it is one hundred percent perfect so that we are no longer sick.

What we need to do is tune into the individual and work together to find their special note for the Thymus, to sound it with loving care and reverence, for a certain number of days. This note may very well be the note F of G, but not necessarily."

"Where then does Sound come into healing the Thymus Chakra and Immune System?"

According to Renee Brodie, *"The Thymus chakra responds to all sounds made by you, and any with which you are in contact. There is much sensitivity in the area of the Thymus chakra because of the bony structure that overlays it. When you sing or shout, pray or chant, or listen to music, whether it be recorded or played live by many musicians, the Thymus chakra is stimulated. From here is directed renewed energy as a result of the sound.*

All sounds, in one way or another, resonate with this chakra and in the body. Now that you are aware of the Thymus chakra, it is so necessary to make joyful, positive sounds instead of "sour" notes of anger or negativity. Awareness of with which sounds one is resonating is very important. Think about the words that we use. Think about the words and sounds that are produced by people who are with you. What are they saying? Are they words of love and caring, of honesty and truth? Is there joy in the sounds that you are using and hearing? Is your personal sound critical and deadening to others? Are you saying things that are uplifting? Do the sounds of everyday life resonate to your beingness? Listen to yourself and learn. You are in charge, one hundred percent, of the sounds that you live with and make, not of the "outside" sounds but of your own sounds, the sounds in your home, office and healing centers, the sounds that you make to your family and friends.

From now on we can all take a little care "cleaning up" the sounds that we make, even to the extent of listening to the tones of our own voices , creating a more beautiful, resonant sound. Bless yourselves, and ask for perfection in creating a blissful, caring and beautiful surrounding of sound.

The Thymus chakra responds to sound, but the whole body, mind and spirit needs peaceful and lovely sounds to create a space in which we can move forward into the full Light."

Through the use of Holographic Sound Healing techniques, all the seven major body chakras plus one major chakra are cleared, balanced and energized. The plus one major chakra is an eight chakra called the Thymus chakra which we have discussed here because of its importance in the proper functioning of the Immune System and which is affected greatly during Holographic Sound Healing as the other seven major chakras are healed.

According to Chinese medicine, The **Heart chakra controls the heart and the thymus gland**, so it is important to focus on this Heart point during meditation to strengthen these organs.

Quartz Crystal Singing Bowls:
Powerful Instruments for Sound Healing & Well-Being

"The use of the bowls is a very sacred act in a way, for you are sounding a note into the Universe, and it reverberates around you, your home, your environment, and ripples out into the world as we know it, also touching others everywhere, and touching other wavelengths of all the invisible ways, altering them for good. Remember this as you sound a Bowl – have only the best intentions within your heart center."

- Renee Brodie, Healing Tones of Crystal Bowls

The following information on Quartz Crystal Singing bowls is derived from Discoverthesound.com which is relevant to holographic sound healing.

Have you ever run your wet finger around the rim of a wine glass or goblet? It makes a singing sound, which varies depending on the size and thickness of the glass. Try it soon if you have never done this! The rotating pressure from your finger actually starts the glass vibrating, which produces sound.

Quartz crystal singing bowls work on the same principle. With the bowls, you use a suede-covered mallet, instead of your finger. You circle this mallet around the outside rim of the bowl, and an enchanting sound begins almost immediately. This tone continues to resonate long after you stop circling with the mallet.

For sound to be produced, something must be vibrating and moving the air. This is easy to see when a harp string is plucked, or when you are watching a big bass drum. With crystal bowl singing bowls, the sides of the bowls are actually flexing and moving slightly in and out as they are played. You can really feel this when you place your hand on the vibrating bowl.

So that's a little bit about how the singing bowls actually make sound. Now let's take a look at how sound is used in various ways throughout the world.

Many cultures recognize the importance of music and sound as a healing tool. In ancient India, Asia, Africa, Europe, and among the Aboriginals and AmerIndians, the practice of using sound to heal and achieve balance has existed for centuries. The Tibetans still use bells, chimes, bowls, and chanting as the foundation of their spiritual practice. In Bali, the gong and drum are used in ceremonies to uplift and to send messages.

The Australian Aboriginals and Native American shamans use vocal toning and repetitive sounds, along with instruments created from nature, in sacred ceremony to adjust any imbalance of the spirit, emotions or physical being. The priests of ancient Egypt knew how to use vowel sounds to resonate their energy centers or chakras. There is a direct link between different parts of the body and specific sounds. Such a technique appears extremely old, yet healing through sound goes back even further, at least as far back as Atlantis, where the power of sound was combined with the power of crystal.

At the present time, the Native American Hopi prophecy is being fulfilled with the "Coming of the Rainbow People", through the keepers of the crystal bowls. This ancient wisdom has emerged to heal and uplift the consciousness of the universe through pure crystal tone. Edgar Cayce, the American psychic, and Rudolf Steiner, German philosopher, educator and artistic genius, both predicted that "pure tones will be used for healing before the end of this century". Nostradamus foretold the healing of cancer through pure tone by 1998. The pure tones created by crystal bowl music enter as a fulfillment of this prophecy.

Everything in the universe is in a state of vibration, and each object or person has a resonant frequency that is their optimal vibration. The chakras, bones and organs in the body all possess a different resonant frequency. When an organ, or other part of the body, is vibrating out of tune or nonharmoniously, it is called "dis-ease". A body is in a healthy state of being when each cell and each organ create a resonance that is in harmony with the whole being. Vibrational therapy is based on the idea that all illness or disease is characterized by blockage in the channels on some level, such as in acupuncture meridians, arteries, veins, nerves and chakras (energy centers). When there is a blockage, the organ in question stops vibrating at a healthy frequency, and thus it results in some kind of illness. Using sound and light, one can break up, dissolve and remove these blockages that initiate in our light or etheric body. Ultra sound (very high-frequency sound), well-known as a diagnostic tool for fetal development, is also being used to cleanse clogged arteries and break up kidney stones.

The body may be seen as a pattern of visible frequencies that produces an auric color field. The aura changes as it reflects emotional states of consciousness, and thus the physiological status. The appearance of the aura is also conditioned by the qualities and activity of each chakra. A chakra may be underactive, overactive, or blocked. These may be temporary conditions or reflect a more deeply held pattern. For example, sudden emotional stress may drive the solar plexus into overactive churning, whereas long term emotional stress may cause a person to nearly shut down the solar plexus chakra so that the person may avoid feeling any more hurt. Of course, this also means that the person lessens the ability to feel at all, including pleasure.

The sounds of the crystal bowls help balance the chakras in two ways. At the same time that the disharmonious conditions are being adjusted or removed, a sacred space is created for strengthening of the person's Higher Self connection or "Divine Blueprint". When an unbalanced energetic condition is removed, it is always wise to fill the void created with the highest aspect of Source that the person is willing to embrace. The sound waves from the crystal bowls emit a pure holographic template of radiant sound that builds a "Jacob's ladder" to the Divine.

The pure tones of crystal bowls produce a vibrational sound field which resonates the light body energy centers (chakras) and corresponding physical areas. There are seven musical notes that correspond to the seven colors of the rainbow, and these are related to the seven main chakras, which in turn correspond to different areas of the endocrine gland system. A series of pure crystal tone sessions facilitates the rebalancing of each receiver back into an elevated level of etheric radiance. The effects are enhanced because the bowls are made of quartz. Silicon crystal acts as an oscillator, magnifying and transmitting pure tone. This is why pure quartz crystal is used in all the world's most advanced telecommunications systems. Like a powerful radio transmitter, the crystal bowls transmit energy into the atmosphere, filling a person's aura with vibrational radiance which translates into the seven main colors of the rainbow.

As the pure crystal tones affect brain wave activity, one can travel into an altered state of consciousness. As different parts of the brain are affected, it is probable that different hormones and neurochemicals are released that suppress pain, overcome addictions, strengthen willpower, and foster creativity. Eva Rudy Jansen, in her book Singing Bowls (1990). documented the effect of Tibetan metal bowls: "It is possible to record the waves produced by singing bowls. It was found that among the wave patterns of different singing bowls, there is a measurable wave pattern which is equivalent to the alpha waves produced by the brain. These bowls, in particular, instill a sense of deep relaxation and inner space opening up." (page 42)

Each crystal bowl is made of 98.9% silicon quartz. One reason why the pure tones vibrate our body is that it has a natural affinity to quartz. The human body is composed of many crystalline substances - the bones, blood and DNA are crystalline in structure, as well as the liquid crystal-colloidal structure of the brain. Even on a molecular level, our cells contain silica, which balances our electromagnetic energies.

Quartz crystal music holds the vibration of white light, which ultimately refracts into the rainbow and acts directly on our chakras when played. It has the power to bring about a positive shift in our consciousness, and as our awareness expands, we grow close to our original selves and start to reflect the highest radiance in our physical form. Physicists know that quartz is able to maintain the balance of electromagnetic energies between its north and south poles, enabling it to play a key role in timekeeping systems. The same electromagnetic field exists within all life forms. Quartz balances our own electromagnetic energies.

Edward Bach, founder of Bach Flower Remedies, understood that illness reflects disharmony between the physical personality and the soul, and stated that it is easy to cure by balancing the magnetic qualities of the higher subtle bodies. Through pure tone, one can repattern the energy field organization that ultimately affects the cellular expression of disease or wellness. Crystal bowl tones are all the more powerful, as the quartz can be programmed in the same way as any quartz crystal.

Quartz crystal, as a holographic light template, is able to hold, transmit, and receive thought forms. In Healing Sounds: The Power of Harmonics (1992), Jonathan Goldman writes, "The intention behind the sound is of extreme importance. It may, in fact, be as important as the actual sounds that are created." The power of thought is the means by which we create our reality. Nothing can be created unless it is first thought. When using crystal to rebalance, the crystal amplifies the thought programmed within it. The crystal has this amazing property, and thus it can be used to bring out a special feeling or quality in people, and simultaneously release and replace thought forms that are not of the highest radiance for the listener.

Only quartz crystal singing bowls offer this unique quality to the growing family of Soundworkers.

Source: Renee Brodie's "Healing Tones of Crystal Bowls" book

I have been using my Quartz Crystal Singing Bowls with excellent healing and spiritual ascension results during my Holographic Sound Healing meditation, balancing, clearing and healing practices which exponentially amplify my toning, thought forms and Unity holograms.

Meditation & Enlightenment with Quartz Crystals

"What is meditation and how does enlightenment happen?" you might ask.

According to Dr. Richard Gerber, *another more powerful form of inner communication with the Higher Self is* **meditation. Meditation** *clears the mind of conscious thought programs to allow higher vibrational sources of information to enter into the biocomputer for processing and analysis. In addition to allowing access to the Higher Self, the process of meditation causes gradual changes in the subtle-energy anatomy of the human being over a long period of time. Specifically, the chakras are slowly activated and cleared, and the kundalini energies within the root chakra eventually make their climb up the subtle pathways within the spinal cord to reach the crown chakra.*

The real reason to meditate is to achieve **enlightenment. Enlightenment** *might be defined here as a more cosmic or energetic perspective of the structures of consciousness, a feeling of unity with all life forms, and an understanding of the spiritual workings behind physical reality. This higher level of perception will ultimately allow the individual to comprehend the meaning of his or her life in relationship to others and to the universe in general. This is what is referred to as a more cosmic perspective. Meditation may ultimately allow humans to come into closer relationship and greater comprehension of God the Creator.*

In human beings the process of enlightenment is intimately tied to the proper alignment and normal functioning of the major chakras of the body. When all of the major chakras are open and active and when there is adequate etheric vitality in the body, the human being begins to function at optimal levels of health and higher consciousness. Meditation merely amplifies this gradual process of awakening. It accelerates the opening of the chakras and their alignment with the physical and subtle bodies in special ways that devotion and prayer alone do not achieve as quickly and directly.

According to Dr. Richard Gerber's **Vibrational Medicine** book, wherein he stated, *An individual's ability to connect with his or her Higher Self is partly a function of specialized energy links within the crystalline network of the physical body. This crystalline network helps to coordinate the energetic structures of the higher subtle bodies with the consciousness of the physical personality. Gurudas brings out new and important information that may explain certain aspects of right-hemispheric functioning and psi abilities. Psychic abilities are mediated by special biocrystalline and energetic pathways through which the Higher Self may interact with the consciousness of the physical personality. One particular crystalline structure that is important to our psychic receptivity is the pineal gland and, more specifically, the pineal calcification: a crystal that lies in the center of the brain.*

The pineal gland in esoteric literature has long been associated with the third eye. Our early biological ancestors actually had a rudimentary but functional third eye, complete with lens, as exists today within the tuatara (a lizard found in the southern hemisphere). The pineal gland is associated with the phenomenon of light from a variety of different biological and energetic perspectives. This esoteric association of the pineal with the third eye in humans stems from the pineal gland's link with the third eye (or brow) chakra. The pineal gland is linked to the chakra system by way of a special energetic circuit which has developed in human beings over the course of time. The function of this specialized energy system is uniquely involved with raising the energies of the personality toward a higher, more spiritual level of consciousness. In addition, this same energy system is responsible for awakening an individual's full creative and evolutionary potential.

According to the channelled material by Kevin Ryerson from his book **Flower Essences and Vibrational Healing,** *the kundalini activation process utilizes the crystalline circuitry of the body, especially the pineal gland, as well as a special resonant energy reflex arc extending from the coccygeal region to the brain stem. Although energy flow through this pathway is primarily involved with the ascension of the kundalini, it appears that this circuit also functions on a more day-to-day basis to allow us to communicate with our Higher Self.*

***The pineal gland is a crystalline structure that receives information from the soul and subtle bodies**, particularly the astral body. The subtle bodies often act as filters for teachings from the soul and Higher Self. **From the pineal gland information travels to the right** portion of the brain. If there is need to alert the conscious mind to this higher information, it passes through the right brain in the form of dreams. Then the left brain analyzes it to see if the information can be grasped. This often occurs with clear dreams that offer messages. From the left brain information travels through the neurological system, specifically passing through two critical reflex points - the medulla oblongata and the coccyx. **There is a constant state of resonancy along the spinal column between the medulla oblongata and coccyx; properties of the pineal gland resonate between these two points.** Then the information travels to other parts of the body through the meridians and crystalline structures already described. **The life force of vibrational remedies activates this entire procedure.** This is a key process the soul uses to manifest karma in the physical body.*

The crystalline circuitry herein described actually contributes to the physiological basis for the kundalini process. Additionally, this circuit permits the step-down transduction of information from the Higher Self to various levels of awareness experienced by the physical personality. **It is most interesting that the right cerebral hemisphere, working in concert with the pineal, acts as a primary relay point for information moving from the Higher Self to the waking personality.**

"What is the function of quartz crystals in meditation?" you might then ask.

Quartz crystals are amplifiers of the energies of consciousness. The energy taken in from meditative visualizations causes a raising of the vibrational rate of the body and an upliftment of consciousness to higher frequency levels. **Meditative techniques which employ the use of visualization allow one to utilize natural right-hemispheric abilities to link more directly with the quartz crystal.**

"What is Christ Consciousness?" you might ask.

According to Katrina Raphaell's **Crystalline Transmission**, *There is no doubt that Jesus the Christ was a perfected being (as well as several other masters and saints that have lived upon the earth). The life of Jesus Christ exemplified unconditional love. There is no question in my mind that all twelve of his chakras were activated and working in impeccable order. How else could he manifest the miracles and the healing that he did? He lived the reality of The Crystalline Transmission and attempted to teach others how to do so as well. We can further relate if we look at one of Jesus's most famous statements. "I and My Father are One," he said. It is obvious that he was one with his source, which in this context is defined as 'father.' Through the activation of the three transpersonal chakras, each one of us can also become one with that same source. With the simultaneous activation of the Earth Chakra, fully ordained Christhood is achieved and the manifestation of miracles and healing can occur on a mass level.*

The Christ Consciousness is very much associated with the light body and the Soul Star (ninth chakra). It is at this chakra where the universal, omnipresent, omnipotent essence of the Stellar Gateway becomes individualized in the lighted 'Christ Self.' The Soul Star translates that cosmic energy into the Christ Consciousness to be relayed directly into the heart of humanity. Just as Jesus the Christed was a messenger on this planet for that state of being, so can we be. Jesus lived at the beginning of the Age of Pisces and served as a singular example of the reality of the Crystalline Transmission. Now, two thousand years later, as we enter into the Golden Age of Aquarius, that crystalline reality becomes possible for the masses. This is the true meaning of 'the second coming of the Christ.' It is in the inner sanctums of our hearts that the Christ Consciousness, actualized at the Soul Star, finds full expression in the miraculous power of love. As the Christ Consciousness is resurrected within us, the rebirth of total spiritual awareness will take place at the third eye and God's perfect plan will be revealed. As the light body is integrated into the physical body, the living Christ will manifest in glorious creations in our lives.

"What is the Crystalline Transmission all about?" you might then ask.

According to Katrina Raphaell's **Crystalline Transmission** book, _The term "The Crystalline Transmission" is synonymous with "blending spirit and matter" and "living heaven on earth." This state of being is the eventual achievement of our human growth process and what each one of us has the opportunity to personally experience. Yes, history has recorded great individuals such as Akhnaton, Jesus Christ, Buddha, Mohammed, and Gandhi who lived in accordance with divine will and served as examples to us of this possibility. But now, the time demands that a much larger number of people receive their divine inheritance by aligning with their soul's essence and striving to live that truth in all of life's activities. Only then, will spiritual force be transmitted into the essence of the earth's substance to affect all living creatures and make possible planetary transformation._

"What is the light body Katrina Raphaell referred to?" _you might ask._

According to Katrina Raphaell's **Crystalline Transmission** book, _The sun is both spiritual light and material form, the purest manifestation of the oneness of that which is visible with the invisible, of matter and energy. The sun is deified cosmic energy, so are crystals, and potentially, so are we. The true worship of the sun is based upon attunement not only to the light, but to the ultimate essence of all existence: the force behind the force, the impersonal energy of the cosmos. **The sun is the light body of the earth, just as our light bodies exist in the Soul Star region above the tops of our heads.** There are billions of suns, just as there are billions of people. The fact remains that the animating force behind it all, is Divine Presence. That essence can be attuned to and integrated into our twelve chakra system by practicing the ancient common worship of the sun._

The four chakras mentioned are the Earth Star which is situated six inches below our feet, the Causal Chakra which is Du Mo 20 acupuncture point on top of the head area, the Soul Star which is the 9th Chakra six inches above our head, and the Stellar Gateway which is the 10th Chakra one foot above our head.

Future of Human Evolution & Healing with Sound

"The ultimate purpose is to bring you to greater self-empowerment… Those who are rewarded with the understanding that they are called to use Sound as part of their work and who recognizes that call and respond to it, will evolve at a rapid pace. Those of you evolving at this rate will be called one day to represent many people, to represent world gatherings of consciousness, and to change the available frequency with your Sound."

- Barbara Marciniak's Bringers of the Dawn – Teachings from the Pleidians

Edgar Cayce predicted that sound would be the medicine of the future. Within the last decade, the use of sound as a healing modality is coming into more focus in both the scientific and medical communities. I have included the following Quotes from different authors on the future of human evolution and healing with sound.

According to Barbara Marciniak's Bringers of the Dawn – Teachings from the Pleidians book, "Sound carries a certain frequency, and the body recognizes the frequency. The body is keyed to respond to the acceptability of this frequency. The great Master Musicians such as Beethoven and Mozart were coded to bring in information of a stable nature, for they received the harmonics of sound at the time when there was a great darkness over the planet. In order to keep a certain remembrance open in the minds of human race, lower vibratory rates of sound were translated into the minds of these Masters. Sound is going to evolve. Now human beings can become the instruments for Sound through toning. Human beings become the flute, the piano, the oboe, and the tuba. They allow energies to use their physical bodies to make a variety of sounds of which they do not direct or attempt to control the range.

Spirit plays, and human beings simply observe the attendance of the symphony that they and all the others are performing. It is quite profound. These harmonics can be utilized in incredible way, for harmonics can evolve many things. One of the things that is important for utilizing these harmonics is to be very silent once the harmonics are complete. The harmonics alter something, they open the door. Certain combinations of sounds played through the human body unlock information and frequencies of intelligence. Being silent for a long period after the harmonics allows human beings to use their bodies as devices to receive and absorb frequencies and to use the vehicle of breathing to take them into ecstatic state… What you intend to do with sound is of the utmost importance. If you are not clear about your intentions, sound can have a way of enveloping upon itself and growing beyond its original capacity. It doubles and quadruples itself with its own impact. **It is very important for you to have a clear intention of what you plan on doing with sound.**"

According to Renee Brodie, "Sound therapy has evolved and can help us understand our note(s). Through that understanding, each of us can begin to orchestrate with many others around us. It is the idea of letting the people sing – to touch chords in each – to bring true harmony not only to people, but to the very Earth itself, and thus be instruments for transformation. The pathway now is to evolve with sound – of nature, which includes us – and of Music of the Spheres. This includes the harmonies felt when the Crystal Bowls are played.

When we contemplate sound – whether it is from the voice, or instruments, or nature, or from Crystal Bowls – we feel its vibrations, and these are the main vehicles for the effect of sound. It is the vibrations which go forth to sound their notes and touch everyone, everything, everywhere. Those who are called to sound their notes, by whatever means, are like new Creators. They are working with the Higher Beings to create a New Earth and a New Heaven. They are greatly blessed even as they work now."

The truths expressed by the above authors concur with the mission and goal of interdimensional beings such as the Hathors who are Masters of Sound and Love and originators of Holographic Sound Healing as summarized in this book and also the mission of the Ascended Master Lord Sananda as shown below.

Logos: The thought of God coeternal with all heirarchial unfoldments of a Divine Thought-Form. In the Son universe "the Logos as Christ," according to Enoch, as the intradeical and extradeical thought of the Godhead. To be in Christ is to be in the Divine Thoughts revealed by the Father. **Planetary Logos**: According to Enoch, in our system of things the fallen planetary life systems of the logos, viz., fallen divinities of the Adam Kadmon who achieved a false state of "godhood" and, therapy, limit soul growth to the veils of terror and material illusion, so that the soul does not seek Length of Days and Life of Eternity.

"Life lived outside of the awareness of our shared Unity Consciousness
is ultimately painful, distressing and sorrowful." – Unknown

The Long Walk to Freedom

"Our deepest fear is not that we are inadequate. Our deepest fear is that we are powerful beyond measure.

It is our light, not our darkness, that most frightens us. We ask ourselves: "Who am I, to be brilliant, gorgeous, talented, fabulous?" Actually, who are we not to be?

You are a child of God. Your playing small doesn't serve the world. There is nothing enlightened about shrinking so that other people won't feel insecure around you.

We are all meant to shine, as children do. We were born to make manifest the glory of God that is within us. It's not just in some of us; it's in everyone.

And as we let our light shine, we unconsciously give other permission to do the same, As we're liberated from our own fear, our presence automatically liberates others."

Nelson Mandela
The Long Walk to Freedom

NOTE by Ricardo B Serrano: I have asked myself, *"What was the greatest fear I have when I was a child*?" My greatest fear was the fear of darkness or evil spirits which drove me to spiritual search for many years. I remember putting a big cross under my pillow and praying to Archangel Michael for protection before I go bed during my childhood. After learning about the Hologram of Love Merkaba and having personally experienced through the Unity Merkaba and holographic sound meditation the loving presence, guidance and protection of the Hathors, Archangel Michael, Lord Sananda, Mother Mary, Angelic Beings and other Ascended Masters and knowing that God is within me, my fear of darkness or evil spirits has left me forever.

After realizing my multidimensionality and the innate spiritual potential in everyone of us for healing, ascension of consciousness, interdimensional travel, and Self-Mastery through the assistance of the Hathors, freedom is at hand after many years of searching and learning from many meditation masters. When you feel the presence of the Hathors, you may sense their beauty and a perfect expression of unconditional love. You may find them to be very humorous and joyful in nature. We tend to take things a little too seriously. The Hathors have their ways of shifting the energy by injecting humor and laughter into a situation. They are some of the most beautiful and loving beings I have ever had the joy to work with.

New Chakra Found!

The clown scientists have found that all our problems can be placed under one heading. Seriousness. Seriousness is the leading cause of everything from Cancer to Reincarnation.

Scientists from the Clown Academy have already discovered a new source of healing. It is a psychic energy point located between the heart chakra and the throat chakra. It is called the clown chakra.

If people are feeling miserable; if they have financial problems; if their relationship situation is the pits; if they are ill health; if they have a need to sue people; if they find fault with their brother; then obviously their clown chakra is closed.

When this happens, the scientists have observed under a high-powered microscope that the cells of every organ display a sad face; and when the clown chakra is open and functioning normally, the cells display a happy face.

The scientists realized that if a person is ill, it is because his mind has projected guilt onto the cells of his body, and has forced out the love that is normally found within each cell in the body. The cells are therefore saying, "**I Lack Love** or **ILL** for short.

The scientists also discovered that all diseases is due to the fact that the cells are "**out of ease**" or **dis-eased**."

When the clown chakra is opened and working (or rather, playing) properly, the psychic mechanism sucks up misery, pain, anger, resentment, grievances, unhappiness and so on, and converts the energy into tiny red heart-shaped balloons.

The red heart balloon contain God's Love and Joy. These balloons are directed to the "dis-eased" cell or situation, and a happy face appears instantly. When the light enters the darkness, the darkness is gone. Sometimes these red heart balloons are called endorphins, due to the fact that when anyone experiences them the feeling of separation ends – they experience being back home with the Father/Mother and hence are no longer an orphan. This is the well known "**end orphan (endorphin) effect**.

So if you think someone is attacking you. Clown scientists recommend that you visualize sending that person red heart shaped balloons filled with God's Love and Joy.

Remember to keep your clown chakra open and remember to LAUGH! – seriousness causes reincarnation.

Celestial Contacts through Holographic Sound and Merkaba

"Can the Holographic Sound Healing techniques be used for spiritual ascension and Celestial contacts in the fifth dimension as powerfully as the Merkaba activation taught by Master Thoth through Alton Kamadon?" you might have asked many times as I did.

"Because the Holographic Sound techniques make it possible to contain the vibrational tone of Spirit inside the Holographic Light Body, it not only exponentially amplifies the vibration for healing but also for interdimensional travel, manifestation and spiritual ascension," I answered.

The Hathors, Masters of Sound and Love, have formulated this ancient yet new holographic techniques which they termed *"Holographic Sound Healing"* which they themselves have tested for our use in healing, interdimensional travel and spiritual ascension and have channeled them for raising individual and collective vibrational levels of consciousness.

According to Hathor Material, *"The Hathors are an interesting part of our genetic memories. We receive information about them from the grids which created the program which creates our reality. That program is generated from the main crystal in the Great Pyramid which connects to 12 other pyramids that formed a matrix, grid system, when the program was created. This program allows us to tap into our genetic memories of past lives in other programs wherein we encountered higher level beings.*

The Hathors are supposedly a race of beings from the higher dimensions of Venus. They are masters of the grid of sound and tones. With that comes the language of vibration as well as the tones of the Urim and Thumim the breastplate of the high Gods. With that comes the lock and key tones to the dimensional gates and portals."

As taught by the Hathors through the proper use of vowel sounds, crystals, colors, crystal gridwork, holograms of love and thought forms (active visualizations) which activate our chakras and *Sahhu* or *golden light body* to a very great degree, spiritual ascension or celestial contact is made possible.

From my intense spiritual experiences when practicing Holographic Sound Healing techniques, I can vouch that its techniques have the key sound and tones to the dimensional gates and portals for celestial contacts in the fifth dimension.

Holographic Sound, as described by the Hathors, is a merging of sound vibration with holographic energy, bringing sound to its true and natural state of being. *Its application with the Unity Merkaba and understanding the meaning and application of Holographic Sound through the Hathors' energy, Archangel Michael and Mother Mary are the keys to the whole secret to why Holographic Sound Healing works.*

Additional Quotations from the Hathors

Within the sound of your voice are the keys to innumerable worlds.

To the advancing or ascending soul, life events are seen as wondrous and beautiful things for they afford the possibility of healing, and healing the past is crucial to the ascension of consciousness. Therefore, whatever events unfold in your life, embrace them with awareness, compassion and intelligent choice. Don't decry your fate. Accept what happens, not as kind of resignation or "giving in," but rather as an acknowledgement of what is actually occurring. From this "owning" or acceptance of your situation you can move to change those things which are in your power to change.

There are miracles waiting for you when you asked the unasked question, "What can I do here that will serve the greatest good? What can I do here that will serve life's deepest purpose through me?

The Flower of Life (*Merkaba*) is a fundamental pattern that the Universe is laid out on, so even the molecular and atomic grids are laid out in this pattern; therefore, it's the platform that unfolds destiny. It is the blueprint. Without it there would be no manifestation.

Within you is a power and a mystery – the power and mystery of life itself. It is a precious gift that has been given. Cherish it. Honor it. Fathom it with your heart and mind. May you find its Source, and may that Source lift you up into the heavenly realms of consciousness.

The more love that you can generate within yourself, for yourself and others, the greater the healing. Love sets up a harmonic field that cascades into the actual cells of the body and into other consciousness levels of one's being. This love is the one thing that many are striving for, and it is very positive and very effective. By all means continue to do this. Love was the fundamental teaching of Sananda, whom you call Jesus, and also the fundamental teaching of the Buddha. Buddha's pathway was through awareness of the duality called samsara, the illusion, and the connection to that which was behind it – love, compassion and awareness.

Another thing affecting the *Ka* is the type of food that you eat and the type of fluids you drink – for the life-force comes in from many areas. Generally speaking, humans have a tendency to get very agitated when someone tells them what they should do or not do in terms of dietary habits because people have great attachments to food. So we will give you a broad guideline here leaving you to choose your path.

Generally speaking, to build the *Ka,* eating "live" foods will assist the process, but you want to do this in balance. If you're not used to eating live foods – meaning uncooked vegetables and fruits, as well as sprouted grains (and seeds), *slowly begin this change*. Add live foods to your diet in a way that feels comfortable. Adding too much live food, without proper preparation, (i.e., not giving your body a chance to adjust to the higher enzyme levels) can lead to a detoxification crisis. As in all things, moderation is best. Listen carefully to your body, not your personality whims. Your body will tell you what it needs and what is best.

This may seem paradoxical, but when you reach a certain point in consciousness, you can eat anything without negative effects. Ultimately, food has very little to do with spiritual evolution. However, our advice is given for the average person who wishes to strengthen his or her *Ka*. Most people will experience an increase in vitality if they start adding some live foods to the diet. As a general principle, life-force is only increased by other life-forces. Your "fast foods" are dead. And those items you call "convenience foods" generally deplete the *Ka* because they require so many digestive enzymes to process these "dead" food stuffs. You see, *one of the major drains on the pranic fire, on the pranic body, is the digestive process*.

Much *prana* is actually required to digest food, especially meat. What happens is that the *prana* gets stepped-down from the *Ka*'s faster vibratory field into the physical body's digestive process with its system of ductless and ducted glands, requiring many digestive enzymes to be produced and secreted. This is a strain on your energy. So watching what you eat, and eating as purely and cleanly as possible will reinforce the *Ka*. Pure water is also critical, as is exercise. In addition, be around nature as much as possible, breathing fresh air that is unpolluted and allowing yourself to be safely exposed to sunlight, especially through your eyes. This means wearing sunglasses as little as possible unless the Sun is so bright that you really need to protect your eyes. These are just some very simple suggestions to incorporate into your life, should you wish. In no way are we giving medical advice or suggesting unsafe experimentation.

You will find, as you build the *Ka*, the *pranic* force, and as you hold the intention to elevate yourself in consciousness, that you will begin to have intuitions and inner understandings about things that are very valuable. This is called "*gnosis*." *Gnosis* means "knowledge," and it comes as a feeling, a sudden "knowing." *Gnosis*, then is a refinement of your feeling nature which naturally evolves as the Ka is strengthened, and which provides a deeper soul connection.

- Excerpts from the *Hathor Material* by Tom Kenyon and Virginia Essene, 1996.

NOTE by Ricardo B Serrano, R.Ac. : *Dr. Johanna Budwig's Diet Protocol* – especially cottage cheese and flax seed soil – elaborated on page 106 after the Episode of this book, will *build the Ka, the pranic body,* and *Jing* (essence) by supplying the body's needed essential fatty acids (*EFAs*) and enzymes of live foods lacking in the standard high fat diet nowadays – fried foods – that is high in *trans-fatty acids and low in EFAs with the attendant effects on health.*

The last of the points mentioned by Dr Budwig from her books and maybe the most important, is the electrons in our food serve as the resonance system for the sun's energy and are truly the element of life. Man acts as an antenna for the sun. The interplay between the photons in the sunbeams and the electrons in the seed oils and our foods, governs all the vital functions of the body.

This has to be one of the greatest discoveries ever made as this combination promotes healing in the body of chronic and terminal diseases. In her book Dr Budwig states "Various highly trained and educated individuals are dismayed and irritated by the fact that serious medical conditions can be cured by cottage cheese and flaxseed oil."

The mixing of the oil and cottage cheese allows for the chemical reaction to take place between the sulfur protein in the cottage cheese and the oil, which makes the oil water soluble for easy absorption into your cells.

Qigong and Holographic Sound Healing

"In the practice of Tai Chi Chi Kung, the increased energy flow developed through the Microcosmic Orbit is integrated into ordinary movement, so that the body learns more efficient ways of utilizing energy in motion. Improper body movements restrict energy flow causing energy blockages, poor posture, and in some cases, serious illness. Quite often, back problems are the result of improper posture, accumulated tension, weakened bone structure, and psychological stress."

- Master Mantak Chia, Awaken Healing Light of the Tao

As a Qi-Healer or Qi Gong Master, I recommend Chinese tonic herbs with Dr. Budwig's diet to build the Three Treasures *Jing* (essence), *Qi* and *Shen*, and practice Siddha meditation (passive yin Qi exercise), Sun Do lower dantian breathing with active yang physical movements, moving meditation such as Pan Gu Shen Gong, Primordial Wuji Qigong, Tibetan Shamanic Qigong, Maitreya (Shiva) Shen Gong, and Sheng Zhen Qigong after doing the Holographic Sound Healing meditation techniques to circulate, preserve, and store the vital life force energy (acquired Qi) generated during Holographic Sound Healing meditation.

Adding Qi Gong movements to the activation of chakras, dantians (lower, middle and upper dantians), color, sound, merkaba, crystal bowl, and crystals of Holographic Sound healing completes the circulation of energy in our Pranic body (*Ka*) thereby strengthening and grounding it to Mother Earth's energy further. Furthermore, these integrated system builds your *Sahhu* or *immortal golden lightbody* for true spiritual immortality which is continuity of consciousness after transition (physical death).

I am recommending my clients to learn these particular Qi Gong forms and techniques together with Holographic Sound Healing and Microcosmic Orbit meditation to further enhance their body's own self-healing power, cultivate the Three Treasures Jing, Qi and Shen, strengthen the immune system, become rooted to earth's energy and balance, clear and heal the chakras, dantians and energy channels (meridians) of the body through **Color, Sound, Merkaba and Qi Movement.** *Sun gazing* is another powerful way to build the *Ka* and can be used together with Qigong and meditation for healing and enlightenment.

According to the Hathors, "There are methods that have been developed by the Taoist sages and tantric yogis which allow you to experience profound states of sexual bliss without depleting the *Ka*. In fact, these practices strengthen the life-force and elevate consciousness. We suggest you explore these methods."

According to Renee Brodie, *"We need to work on the idea of marrying **sound and colour and movement.** In truth, the three are not really separate, but work together, complementing each other to make us whole. This means that the colour (of a high vibration) is connected with Light and affects the higher subtle bodies. It touches the soul body and higher mental body. When we join colour with sound, the latter reaches the emotional and lower mental bodies. Add to these two the movement (of Chi through the practice of Tai Chi or Qi Gong), and this then touches the physical and etheric bodies. Why chi? Because it reaches into all the meridians (as opposed to dance, which touches vibrations, but not as deeply as chi energy - essential energy of living organisms and the Universe)."*

KA (MERKABA) MEDITATION PROCEDURE
According to the HATHORS

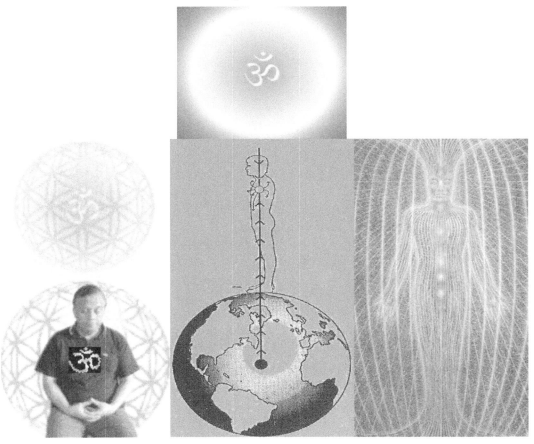

- Invoke the presence of the Hathors, Buddhas, Bodhisattvas, and ascended masters for assistance, protection, healing, guidance and support of this lightbody activation.
- Focus your breathing on your lower dantian (1.5 inches below navel) to calm you down.
- Open your heart and send a golden beam of light radiating from your heart to the pranic tube or central pillar, and from your heart up to Ka of the Sun and from your heart to the heart of Earth.
- Visualize a beautiful and radiant sphere of light (Merkaba) all around you. This is your lightbody. The center of the sphere is aligned with your heart. Its energy extends all the way around your body and moves all the way inwards to the core of your heart.
- Fill this sphere of light with the most divine and unconditional love and light from Ka of the Sun and Earth into your heart and see this sphere filling with love.
- A most radiant Ka (Merkaba) manifests in the center of this space, rotating clockwise God speed and pulsating.
- Now see the sphere of light transforming into a beautiful hologram of love with the petals forming a perfect flower of life sphere.
- Tune into it, sense and feel its softness and its vitality.
- See this Hologram of Love transforming into a Holomatrix of Love with multiple holograms. Draw into your body the infinite wisdom and love and power from your lightbody. Sense and feel the love and light within your being.
- The divine vibration of EL-KA-LEEM-OM is incorporated into your Ka or Merkaba (Lightbody) by chanting the mantra of the Four Sacred Elements within the sacred space of your heart.

For a more guided Ka (Merkaba) activation, view the Omkabah Heart Lightbody Activation video

The Self is of the nature of the Syllable Om. – Mandukya Upanishad 1.8.12

OUR SUN'S SOLAR KA BODY

BY TOM KENYON
WWW.TOMKENYON.COM

Our Sun's Solar Ka Body

Your Sun, the solar star of your planetary system, is increasing its energetic potential and is entering a period of increased volatility, solar flares and magnetic storms.

While these actions will create real problems for you in terms of your ***telecommunications and weather patterns***, there is also **an immense evolutionary potential within this solar activity** that we wish to discuss.

Like you, your Sun has an etheric body, a solar KA, if you will.

This etheric body of the Sun extends millions of miles beyond the boundaries of the Sun itself.

Your Earth is well within this auric field of the etheric sun, and, as the solar flares and solar winds that drive charged particles through your vicinity affect you physically, they also affect you etherically.

Indeed, these very charged particles that pose a challenge to your physical dimension are a type of nourishment for your KA, your own etheric body.

Your mental attitude and emotional/vibratory state is what determines whether these solar particles are a source of nourishment and evolution, or rather a source of annoyance and de-evolution.

In this message we do not intend to discuss the many physical challenges that will emerge for you during this period of increased solar activity, *rather we will focus on things that will assist you to take the greatest evolutionary advantage of what is occurring with the Sun of your solar system.*

Just as there are *eruptions of fire and photonic energy from the Sun during solar activity*, so too, there are *bursts of spiritual or interdimensional light from within your KA body*.

Indeed, from one perspective, increased solar activity equates with an increased activation of your own personal KA.

These are distinct flows of photonic and magnetic energy that pass through and around your Earth.

By opening yourself to these distinct forms of energy, and by incorporating them into your KA body, you strengthen your KA and greatly accelerate the ascension process for yourself.

As these solar energies increase, so will the volatility and uncertainty of your physical world, as well as your mental and emotional worlds.

Irrationality and impulsive behavior will be on the rise. Challenges to cognitive functioning and memory will also take place during heightened cycles of solar activity.

The first step *in utilizing these solar energies for your ascent in consciousness is to understand their nature and not to resist their effects.*

It is important to understand that the causative agent in the increased solar activity at this time is not originating from within the Sun itself, but rather it is originating from the Central Sun of your own galaxy.

This flow of highly catalytic energies from the Central Sun to your Sun is the primary reason for the evolutionary potentials of this particular cycle of solar activity.

In turn, the Earth herself is also being affected, especially through her KA—her own etheric body.

So the first thing to understand is that **there is no escape from this evolutionary catalyst.** You are here to ride it out, whether you like it or not.

So the first step is **not to resist that which is imminent.**

The second step is *to embrace it* *and to utilize these energies with mastery—to ride the tail of the dragon, so to speak.*

In this instance, ***the dragon is referring to the Sun itself and the tail to the solar winds.***

You can ascend to great heights in this period, if you but find the courage and method to do so.

The third step *in this utilization of the solar winds is to* allow them to affect your KA directly, through an invitation, and this is done through your heart.

Specifically you choose, through an act of personal will, to enter into the vibrational harmonic of appreciation or gratitude.

It is important to understand why we are suggesting this. You are not expressing appreciation or gratitude to the universe for the solar winds, per se.

You are choosing to enter into one of these high emotional states because they will create an **Energy Attractor.**

In other words, you are entering into a state of appreciation or gratitude for pragmatic reasons.

These emotional states increase the receptive harmonics of your KA, which transforms your entire KA body into a receptive vortex, drawing to itself the photonic and magnetic energies of the Sun, rapidly accelerating the rate of vibration within your KA, your own etheric body.

And it is through your KA that you enter into the ascension process. There are, needless to say, many paths and ways to enter the ladder that leads upward into higher states of consciousness, but regardless of how it is done, or through what spiritual lineage it is accomplished, **the KA, your KA, is the foundation.**

In this simple but highly effective method, you place your awareness in your second body, your KA.

This energy body is the same shape and size as your physical body, but it is energetic in nature, rather than made of flesh and blood. It permeates every space of your body, and thus every cell of your body is within the KA.

Your KA is also highly receptive to subtle energies especially to all forms of light and to the charged photons and magnetic energies that comprise the solar winds.

As you rest your awareness in your KA, you consciously and intentionally generate the feeling-state of appreciation or gratitude through an act of personal will.

This shifts the harmonics of your KA to a higher vibratory rate, which is necessary for it to become an Energy Attractor.

As you continue to hold yourself in the emotional harmonic of appreciation or gratitude, know (realize) that you are immersed in the photonic and subtle energies of the solar winds.

You are literally bathing in these energies whether you are consciously aware of them or not.

As you hold this awareness, along with the emotional state of appreciation or gratitude, your KA will automatically draw into itself the ascension-enhancing energies of the solar winds.

Spend as long as you can in this state of high receptivity, partaking from the solar winds, and allowing your KA to receive these potent transformational and uplifting energies.

You will benefit greatly from the solar winds if you regularly and often engage this simple method.

Excerpts from Tom Kenyon's channelled message from the Hathors, January 3, 2011

Quotations on the Ka of the Sun

Ka of the Sun

It is true to say that "the old Heliopolitan traditions made Tem-Ra, or Khepera, the creator of Aten (the Disk), but this view Amenhotep the Fourth rejected, and he asserted that the Disk was self-created and self-subsistent." This statement is all the more significant because it comes from a scholar who, far from being one of Akhnaton's admirers, has never lost an opportunity to minimise the importance of his Teaching. Here, the enormous gap between the Religion of the Disk and the old Heliopolitan cult, its historic ancestor, is emphasised without the learned author seeming to suspect what a homage he is paying, indirectly, to the young Pharaoh's genius. For if the object of the latter's adoration were purely "the heat and light," or energy within the Disk, then one fails to understand why he rejected the view of the priests of On about a god separate from the Disk and creator of it — a god of whom Shu (the heat and light) is an emanation, in the same manner as Shu's female counterpart, Tefnut, the goddess of Moisture. And if, on the contrary, the object of his worship were the material Disk itself and nothing more, then why should he have called it "Shu-which-is-in-the-Disk"? Moreover, why should he say in the short hymn: "At Thy rising, all hands are lifted in adoration of Thy Ka"? And, again, in the long hymn, speaking this time of the worship of the Sun, not by men, but by birds: "The feathered fowl fly about over the marshes, praising Thy Ka with their wings"? In the case of a living being its "Ka" designates its double, or soul; that invisible element of it which survives death; its subtle essence as opposed to its coarser visible body. The "Ka" of the Sun would therefore be the Sun's soul, so as to say; the subtle principle which is the essence of the Sun, and which would survive the material Disk, were it one day to decay and pass away — the eternal Sun, as opposed to the visible Sun.

We believe that the best way to account for this apparent ambiguity is to admit that Akhnaton worshipped the Radiant Energy of the Sun as the Principle of all existence on earth, but deliberately brushed aside the Heliopolitan distinction between the god, maker of the solar Disk, and the solar Disk itself, the distinction between creative energy and created matter. To him — and in this we cannot but admire one of the traits of his far-seeing genius — there was no such distinction. To him the Disk was self-created and self-sustaining, because it was, like all matter that falls under our senses, but a visible manifestation of Something more subtle, invisible, intangible, everlasting — its "Ka" or essence. And Shu, the heat and light, the energy of the Sun, was not the emanation from the body of a god different from it, but the manifestation of that One Thing which the visible flaming Disk was another manifestation. It was the Disk itself, and the Disk was it. Visible Matter was not the product of Energy, distinct from it, nor Energy the product of Matter, distinct from it; nor were any particular forms of Energy, such as heat and light, the products of any creative power distinct from them by nature. But, as was to be suggested thirty-three hundred years later by the inquiries of the modern scientists into the structure of the atom, Matter and Energy were inseparable, and both everlasting; they were one. To maintain the distinctions put forward in olden days by the priests of the Sun in On — the distinction between the creator of the Disk and the Disk itself, and also between both these and the Heat and Light within the Disk — was to deny, or at least to hide, the secret identity of the visible and invisible Sun, of the visible and invisible world, of Energy and Matter.

That identity, Akhnaton had become aware of through some mysterious inner experience of which history has not preserved any description, and by which he transcended the human to reach the cosmic scale of vision. It is probable that he could not explain it, as the scientists of our age do, in terms of definite patterns of energy. But he knew it, none the less, to be the objective truth. And, anticipating in a tremendous intuition the rational conclusions of modern research, he based his religion upon the three ideas that summarise them, namely:

1. The essential equivalence of all forms of energy, including that yet to-day unanalyzed (and perhaps unanalyzable) form which is life;
2. The essential identity of matter and energy, each of the two being but the subtler or the coarser aspect of the other;
3. The indestructible existence, without beginning, without end, of that One unknown Thing, which is Matter to the coarser and Energy to the finer senses.

The "Ka" of the Sun, mentioned in the hymns, must indeed be taken to mean the soul or essence of our parent star. And it seems certain that the immediate object to which the king's followers were invited to offer their praise was not the material Disk alone, as some critics have supposed, nor the "Ka" of the Disk regarded as distinct from it, but the Disk with its "Ka," regarded as one; the Sun, body and soul, visible and invisible, matter and energy; the dazzling Orb itself being, as we have just remarked, but what our senses can perceive, at our ordinary scale of vision, of the enormous store of Radiant Energy that gave birth to our planet and all it contains, and continues to keep it alive.

In the hymns, it is repeatedly stated that Aton is "one" and "alone." It is said, for instance, in the short hymn, "Thou Thyself art alone, but there are millions of powers of life in Thee to make them (Thy creatures) live," and again in the other hymn, "O Thou One God, like unto Whom there is no other, Thou didst create the earth according to Thy heart (or will), Thou alone existing."

It is true that the worshippers of every great god in Egypt had from time immemorial declared that their god was "one" even while they themselves admitted the existence of different gods. We find the expression "one" and "alone" in older anonymous hymns to Amon, to Ra, to Tem, and other deities, long before Akhnaton. And it is also true that "it was obvious that Aten, the solar Disk, was one alone and without counterpart or equal." But if we see, as it seems we should, in Akhnaton's identification of the solar Disk with its "Ka" or essence the sign of his belief in the oneness of invisible Energy and visible Matter, then the words "one" and "alone," when used by him, become more than casual utterances. They express the only knowable attribute of that supreme entity, Substance and Power at the same time, which is at the back of all existence; they qualify the essence of all suns — the universal "Ka" — not only the essence of our Sun. For these are the same. And whether Akhnaton personally knew or not of the existence of other suns besides the one that rules the life of our earth, it makes little difference. His religion bears from the start the character of the broadest and most permanent scientific truth, embracing, along with the reality of our solar system, that of all existing systems; nay, of all possible systems.

The text of the hymns refers to no legends, to no stories, to no particular theogony; only to the beauty and beneficence of our parent star, to its light "of several colours," to its universal worship by men, beasts and the vegetable world; to the marvel of birth; to the joy of life; to the rhythm of day and night and of the seasons, determined by the Sun; and to the great idea that the heat and light within the solar-disk, the "Ka" or Soul of the Disk, and the Disk itself, are one, and that all creatures are one as the children of the one Sun — the one God. We find here nothing but conceptions that need, in order to be accepted, only common sense and sensitiveness to beauty; and in order to be understood in their full, not a theological but a rational — and also spiritual — preparation; not the knowledge of any mythology or even of any human history, but a scientific knowledge of the universe, coupled with a spirit of synthesis.

It seems, from this prayer addressed to the One God, that Akhnaton believed in the survival of the individual soul after death. The "I" who speaks here is, or at least has all the appearances of being, a personal consciousness. But it is difficult to imagine personal consciousness beyond death without some sort of survival of the body. We all feel that we owe much of what we are to the characteristic constitution of our various organs. If nothing is to remain of our material self under any form, then the only sort of immortality we can expect, if any at all, is the impersonal immortality of that which is, in us, common to all beings; substantial everlastingness, rather than individual immortality. Akhnaton seems to have been aware of this, and not to have separated the survival of the individual from some sort of hazy corporeality. At least, that is what we would imagine to be implied in words such as: ". . . that my limbs may be rejuvenated with life through love of Thee."

No one can say whether those very same words also imply that the Founder of the Religion of the Disk shared the age-old Egyptian belief in the resurrection of the dead. It may be he did. It may be he did not. It may be that, in his eyes, the "limbs" that constitute, in eternity, the agent of individualisation, were those not of the resurrected mummy but of some surviving "body" more subtle than the visible one. In Akhnaton's conception, as it can be inferred from the hymns, there is, as we have seen, no clear-cut line of demarcation between the material and the immaterial — between the everlasting "Ka" of the Sun-disk and the Disk itself, and doubtless also between the immortal "ka" of a man — his subtler self — and that man's body.

Thus Akhnaton loved the world of forms because it is beautiful, and, through it, soon grasped and loved the eternal beauty of the unseen world of essences. The splendour of the Disk that rises and sets led him to the worship of the "Ka" of the Disk, the supreme Essence. When, a thousand years later, Plato put forward, in immortal language, his famous dialectic of love — the glorious ascension of the enraptured soul from beautiful forms to beautiful Ideas, everlasting prototypes of all that appears for a while in the phenomenal play — he expressed nothing else but that which the youthful Founder of the Religion of the Disk had once realised, lived and taught.

- Excerpts from Son of the Sun: The Life and Philosophy of Akhnaton, King of Egypt by Savitri Devi, 1946.

With thanks and acknowledgement to the late Savitri Devi for the excerpts at www.savitridevi.org

HYMNS TO THE SUN
BY AKHNATON
WWW.SAVITRIDEVI.ORG

LONGER HYMN

Thy appearing is beautiful in the horizon of heaven,
The Living Aten[1], the beginning of life;
Thou risest in the horizon of the east,
Thou fillest every land with thy beauty.

Thou art very beautiful, brilliant and exalted above earth,
Thy beams encompass all lands which thou hast made.
Thou art the sun, thou settest their bounds,
Thou bindest them with thy love.
Thou art afar off, but thy beams are upon the land;
Thou art on high, but the day passes with thy going.

Thou restest in the western horizon of heaven,
And the land is in darkness like the dead.

They lie in their houses, their heads are covered,
Their breath is shut up, and eye sees not to eye;
Their things are taken, even from under their heads, and they know it not.

Every lion cometh forth from his den,
And all the serpents then bite;
The night shines with its lights,
The land lies in silence;
For he who made them is in his horizon.

The land brightens, for thou risest in the horizon,
Shining as the Aten in the day;
The darkness flees, for thou givest thy beams,
Both lands are rejoicing every day.

Men awake and stand upon their feet,
For thou liftest them up;
They bathe their limbs, they clothe themselves,
They lift their heads in adoration of thy rising,
Throughout the land they do their labours.

The cattle all rest in their pastures,
Where grow the trees and herbs;
The birds fly in their haunts,
Their wings adoring thy ka,
All the flocks leap upon their feet,
The small birds live when thou risest upon them.

The ships go forth north and south,
For every way opens at thy rising.
The fishes in the river swim up to greet thee,
Thy beams are within the depth of the great sea.

Thou createst conception in women, making the issue of mankind;
Thou makest the son to live in the body of his mother,
Thou quietest him that he should not mourn,
Nursing him in the body, giving the spirit that all his growth may live.
When he cometh forth on the day of his birth,
Thou openest his mouth to speak, thou doest what he needs.

The small bird in the egg, sounding within the shell,
Thou givest to it breath within the egg,
To give life to that which thou makest.
It gathers itself to break forth from the egg,
It cometh from the egg, and chirps with all its might,
It runneth on its feet, when it has come forth.

How many are the things which thou hast made!
Thou createst the land by thy will, thou alone,
With peoples, herds and flocks,
Everything on the face of the earth that walketh on its feet,
Everything in the air that flieth with its wings.

In the hills from Syria to Kush, and the plain of Egypt,
Thou givest to every one his place, thou framest their lives,
To every one his belongings, reckoning his length of days;
Their tongues are diverse in their speech,
Their natures in the colour of their skin.
As the divider thou dividest the strange peoples.

When thou hast made the Nile beneath the earth,
Thou bringest it according to thy will to make the people to live:
Even as thou hast formed them unto thyself,
Thou art throughout their lord, even in their weakness.
O lord of the land that risest for them.

Aten of the day, revered by every distant land, thou makest their life,
Thou placest a Nile in heaven that it may rain upon them,
That it may make waters upon the hills like the great sea,
Watering their fields amongst their cities.
How excellent are thy ways!

O Lord of eternity, the Nile in Heaven is for the strange people,
And all wild beasts that go upon their feet.
The Nile that cometh from below the earth is for the land of Egypt,
That it may nourish every field.
Thou shinest and they live by thee.

Thou makest the seasons of the year to create all thy works;
The winter making them cool, the summer giving warmth.
Thou makest the far-off heaven, that thou mayest rise in it,
That thou mayest see all that thou madest when thou wast alone.

Rising in thy forms as the living Aten,
Shining afar off and returning.
The villages, the cities, and the tribes, on the road and the river,
All eyes see thee before them,
Thou art the Aten of the day over all the land.

Thou art in my heart, there is none who knoweth thee, excepting thy son Nefer .
kheperu . ra .ua . en . ra;
Thou causest that he should have understanding, in thy ways and in thy might.

The land is in thy hand, even as thou hast made them;
Thou shinest and they live, and when thou settest they die;
For by thee the people live, they look on thy excellencies until thy setting;
They lay down all their labours when thou settest in the west,
And when thou risest, they grow. . . .
Since the day that thou laidest the foundations of the earth,
Thou raisest them up for thy son who came forth from thy substance,
The king of Egypt, living in Truth, lord of both lands, Nefer . kheperu . ra . ua . en . ra,
Son of the sun, living in Truth, Akhenaten, great in his duration; Nefer . neferu . Aten
Nefer . iti, living and flourishing for ever eternally.

Translated by Griffith, quoted by Sir Flinders Petrie in *A History of Egypt* (Edit. 1899), Vol. II, pp. 215-218.

SHORTER HYMN

A Hymn of Praise to the living Horus of the Two Horizons, who rejoiceth in the horizon in his name of "Shu, who-is-in-the-Aten" (*i.e.*, Disk), the Giver of Life for ever and ever, by the King who liveth in Truth, the Lord of the Two Lands, NEFER-KHEPERU-RA UA-EN-RA, Son of Ra, who liveth in Truth, Lord of the Crowns, AAKHUNATEN, great in the duration of his life, Giver of Life for ever and ever.

(He saith)

Thou risest gloriously, O thou Living Aten, Lord of Eternity! Thou art sparkling (or coruscating), beautiful, (and) mighty. Thy love is mighty and great . . . thy light, of diverse colours, leadeth captive (or, bewitcheth) all faces. Thy skin shineth brightly to make all hearts to live. Thou fillest the Two Lands with thy love, O thou god, who did(st) build (thy)self. Maker of every land, Creator of whatsoever there is upon it, (viz.) men and women, cattle, beasts of every kind, and trees of every kind that grow on the land. They live when thou shinest upon them. Thou art the mother (and) father of what thou hast made; their eyes, when thou risest, turn their gaze upon thee. Thy rays at dawn light up the whole earth. Every heart beateth high at the sight of thee, (for) thou risest as their Lord.

Thou settest in the western horizon of heaven, they lie down in the same way as those who are dead. Their heads are wrapped up in cloth, their nostrils are blocked, until thy rising taketh place at dawn in the eastern horizon of heaven. Their hands then are lifted up in adoration of thy Ka; thou vivifiest hearts with thy beauties (or, beneficent acts), which are life. Thou sendest forth thy beams, (and) every land is in festival. Singing men, singing women (and) chorus men make joyful noises in the Hall of the House of the Benben Obelisk, (and) in every temple in (the city of) Aakhut-Aten, the Seat of Truth, wherewith thy heart is satisfied. Within it are dedicated offerings of rich food (?).

Thy son is sanctified (or, ceremonially pure) to perform the things which thou willest, O thou Aten, when he showeth himself in the appointed processions.

Every creature that thou hast made skippeth towards thee, thy honoured son (rejoiceth), his heart is glad, O thou Living Aten, who (appearest) in heaven every day. He hath brought forth his honoured son, UA-EN-RA, like his own form, never ceasing so to do. The son of Ra supporteth his beauties (or beneficent acts).

NEFER-KHEPERU-RA UA-EN-RA (saith)

I am thy son, satisfying thee, exalting thy name. Thy strength (and) thy power are established in my heart. Thou art the Living Disk, eternity is thine emanation (or, attribute). Thou hast made the heavens to be remote so that thou mightest shine therein and gaze upon everything that thou hast made. Thou thyself art Alone, but there are millions of (powers of) life in thee to make them (*i.e.*, thy creatures) live. Breath of life is it to (their) nostrils to see thy beams. Buds burst into flower (and) the plants which grow on the waste lands send up shoots at thy rising; they drink themselves drunk before thy face. All the beasts frisk about on their feet; all the feathered fowl rise up from their nests and flap their wings with joy, and circle round in praise of the Living Aten. . . .

Translated by Sir E. Wallis Budge, in *Tutankhamen, Amenism, Atenism, and Egyptian Monotheism*, London, 1923, pp. 116-135.

Excerpts from *Savitri Devi's* book *Son of the Sun*, 1956

NOTE by Ricardo B Serrano: Akhnaton (Egyptian name meaning *Joy of the Sun*) has become a blissful self-realized person through worshipping the visible disk of the Sun – Aten, "*the Energy within the Disk*" – the ultimate Reality which men of all creeds still seek under different names and through many paths, when he styled himself as the Son of the God Source of all life, health and joy (love). "*Thou art in my heart*," he said in his hymn to the Sun, "*and no one knoweth Thee save I, Thy Son*."

The idea of his own oneness with the supreme immanent Reality – solar Energy, i.e., Cosmic Energy – was the result of Akhnaton's inner experience – an experience as compelling and, to the person who lived it, by no means more "irrational" than any sensous apprehension of facts, and shared by all those whom we call "*realised*" or "*God-conscious*" souls.

By living in truth, he may have meant that in Atenism he had found the truth or the 'real' thing, and that all else, in religion, was a phantom, a sham. Aten lived in *maat*, or in truth and reality, and the king, having the essence of Aten in him, did the same. – *Savitri Devi, Son of the Sun*

He was a thinker, an artist, a saint – the world's first rationalist, the oldest Prince of Peace, the first sunlight therapist, a sun gazer and sun-worshipper, and the Great Grand Master of the Great White Brotherhood. He was spoken of as "beloved of Thoth," god of wisdom.

The Emerald Tablets of Thoth the Atlantean

The great search for light, life and love only begins on the material plane. Carried to its ultimate, its final goal is complete oneness with the universal consciousness. The foundation in the material is the first step; then comes the higher goal of spiritual attainment.

Concealed in the words of Thoth are many meanings that do not appear on the surface. Light of knowledge brought to bear upon the Tablets will open many new fields for thought. "Read and be wise" but only if the light of your own consciousness awakens the deep-seated understanding which is an inherent quality of the soul. -- Introduction & Translation by Doreal

Tablet 11 Key to Above and Below

List ye, now to my voice and become
greater than common man.
Lift thine eyes upward,
let *Light* fill thy being,
be thou ever Children of *Light*.
Only by effort shall ye grow upward to
the plane where *Light* is the All of the All.
Be ye the master of all that surrounds thee.
Never be mastered by the effects of thy life.
Create then ever more perfect causes
and in time shalt thou be a *Sun of the Light.*

Free, let thine soul soar ever upward,
free from the bondage and fetters of night.
Lift thine eyes to the *Sun* in the sky-space.
For thee, let it be a symbol of *Life*.
Know that thou art the *Greater Light*,
perfect in thine own sphere,
when thou art free.
Look not ever into the blackness.
Lift up thine eyes to the space above.
Free let thine *Light* flame upward
and shalt thou be a *Child of the Light*.

Medicines of Light

The central message here is that all human beings have the ability to create what the Hathors call *Medicines of Light*. And this type of medicine has an inherent capability and potential to protect and heal us not only from radioactive poisoning, but also from the effects of neurotoxins, as well as bacterial and viral infections.

The method is simple and to the point. Since some of you reading this may be new to the whole idea of a Celestial Soul (or BA), let me clarify its location and how to engage it. The BA, or Celestial Soul, is an aspect of your own consciousness that is outside the constraints of time and space. Some of you might refer to the Celestial Soul as the Higher Self. But whatever you call it, your Celestial Soul exists in what the Hathors call *the light realms*, and this aspect of you is engaged whenever you send it appreciation or gratitude.

Your BA does not have a location in time and space since it is transcendent to both.

But it does have an entry point to your energy field, which is about arm's distance above your head. If you were to raise your hands over your head and touch your fingertips together, your fingers would be in the vicinity of this entry point. And this is where you place your attention in the first phase of their method for creating a Medicine of Light. (Do note that placing of your hands above your head is only for orientation purposes. You do not actually put your hands over your head when creating the Medicines of Light).

Once you place your awareness in the area of your BA point, you hold in your mind the qualification of light you wish to receive. Let's say, for example, that you have been, or will be, exposed to dangerous forms of radioactivity and are in danger of radiation poisoning. After focusing your attention on your BA point above your head, hold the intent that the energy that descends from your BA will be an energetic of healing and/or protection from radiation poisoning.

You then send the feeling of appreciation or gratitude upward from your heart chakra to the BA point above your head—as you hold the intent or qualification that the energetic imparted to you from your BA will protect and/or heal you from radiation poisoning.

Next you shift your attention from your BA point to your heart chakra (in the center of your chest beneath the sternum) and then wait to receive the energetic of protection and healing from your BA.

Those of you new to this may need to send the intent or qualification along with the feeling of appreciation or gratitude to your BA several times before you notice a response. But just keep sending this intention joined with the feeling of appreciation or gratitude upward to your BA until you feel a descent of energy. When you feel the descent of energy from your Celestial Soul, shift your awareness to your heart chakra. Allow your heart center to receive this energetic of protection and healing.

You then place your hands around or over a container of pure water and send this energetic received from your Celestial Soul into the water. The energetic of healing and/or protection that has entered your heart center will move down your arms and into the water through the two chakras that are in the center of the palm of each hand.

Repeat this process for a total of three times. Then drink the water.

If you are in a precarious situation, the Hathors advise that you create a Medicine of Light several times a day and drink it according to your intuition.

As the Hathors point out, Medicines of Light have many more applications than just protection and healing from radiation poisoning. You can use these to protect and/or heal yourself from neurotoxins, as well as bacterial and viral infections. Although they did not mention it, I asked the Hathors after they gave this message if the method would work for other physical challenges such as cancer. And they said that Medicines of Light could most definitely be created in the same way to deal with this type of situation—as well as others.

Obviously, if you are dealing with a serious situation such as radiation poisoning, exposure to neurotoxins, and/or epidemics of bacterial and viral infections, you will want to avail yourself of all medical remedies. In other words, this method is not meant to replace medical or public health solutions, but is meant to be an adjunct, something you can do *yourself—for yourself*.

After giving their message, I asked the Hathors about making Medicines of Light for those who are unable to do it for themselves, like children and pets. They said that you would use the same method, except for the fact that you would qualify the intent for the child or animal you are going to give the Medicine to. For example, if you were creating a Medicine of Light to protect or heal yourself from radiation poisoning, you would send the thought that the energetic you are going to receive from your Celestial Soul is for your own personal protection or healing. If you were going to do this for a child or a pet, you would send the thought that the energetic you are going to receive from your Celestial Soul is for the protection or healing of the being you are going to give the Medicine to, i.e. your child or your pet.

It is here that I would like to interject something. It is far better to teach someone how to create a Medicine of Light than to create a dependency. The ability to create Medicines of Light is an inherent ability in all human beings. It is part of our multidimensional legacy. And to empower someone to do this for him or her self is a service to his or her mastery.

I would personally hate to see this method being used by "healers" to create Medicines of Light for others under the guise that they have some special powers that others do not. This method for creating Medicines of Light is a human birthright, and my feeling is that it should be shared with all persons.

There is much that I would like to share about this simple method for creating Medicines of Light, but philosophical and metaphysical observations will have to wait for another time.

The Hathors are insistent that we post this information and circulate it as quickly as is possible.

- Excerpts from Tom Kenyon's Hathors Message March 26, 2011
www.tomkenyon.com

HATHOR MESSAGE on DISTANCE HEALING, NOVEMBER 3, 2011
CHANNELLED THROUGH RICARDO B SERRANO

The *Medicines of Light* technique channelled through Tom Kenyon can also be used to directly heal people that needs one-on-one healing.

Connecting to your pranic tube first, and doing the *Ka (Merkaba) Lightbody Meditation* procedure and connecting your tongue to your palate before doing hands-on-healing on somebody are the only additional practice.

After practicing the *Ka (Merkaba) Lightbody Meditation* with chanting with gratitude four times the *Four Sacred Elements* Mantra – EL-KA-LEEM-OM – you connect with the BA soul center above your head and connect with your heart chakra. Once you feel the connection between the heart and the BA center, you can start distance healing or one-on-one healing with somebody who needs healing, channelling the healing loving energy through both palms of your hands. You can visualize the person you are healing remotely when a person is not in your physical presence.

May you teach and practice this Distance Healing technique for everyone's benefit.

Your loving friends,
Hathors

NOTE by Ricardo B Serrano: This simplified distance healing technique channelled by the Hathors has been an inspiration for me not only because of its simplicity and effectiveness, it also builds your *Sahhu* or *immortal golden lightbody.*

"God consciousness is the reality of everything." – Shiva Sutra 1.1

The chapters covered in this book are the preliminary knowledge from a *pantheistic non-dualistic God concept – God is everything and everything is God –* that needed to be understood before applying the *Distance Healing technique.*

What is Distance Healing and Its Healing Benefits?

*"Distant pranic healing is based on the principle of directability
and the principle of interconnectedness."*

Distance healing is basically healing spiritually someone at a distance or remotely in another location (city, country) by a spiritually developed healer. The date and time for distance healing is synchronized between a client and a healer, so that a client or patient is receptive to a distance healer's Qi-healing. Picture of a patient is helpful to establish a stronger etheric link with a patient.

Why does it work?

The following principles are based on the principles of pranic healing:

Principle of Transmittability. Life force or vital energy can be transmitted from one person to another person.

Principle of Receptivity. A patient has to be receptive or at least neutral to receive the projected pranic energy. Being relaxed also helps increase the degree of receptivity. Without receptivity, the projected pranic energy will not be absorbed, or only a minimal amount of it will be absorbed. Patients may not be receptive because: they are biased towards this type of healing, they do not like the healer personally, they do not want to get well, or they are in general not receptive about anything.

Principle of Interconnectedness. The body of the patient and the body of the healer are interconnected with each other since they are part of the earth's energy body. On a more subtle level, it means that we are part of the solar system. We are interconnected with the whole cosmos. The principle of interconnectedness is also called the *Principle of Oneness*.

Principle of Directability. Life force can be directed. It follows where attention is focused; it follows thought. Distant pranic healing is based on the principle of directability and the principle of interconnectedness.

Source: Advanced Pranic Healing by Master Choa Kok Sui, 1992.

Healing Benefits of Distance healing

The same physical, psychological and emotional healing benefits are obtained in distance healing as in a regular one-on-one Qi-healing session. Most clients have noted that their spirits have lifted with an overall experience of tingling all over the body, inner peace, psychological and emotional healing. Some clients have noted that they felt lightness, revitalized, energized and joyful.

"Love is the most powerful energy for health and healing."

Conclusion:

Regular one-on-one pranic or Qi-healing session is generally a preferable mode of healing, however, because of distance and time restraints between a healer and a patient, distance healing is another viable option to those who prefer remote distance healing.

Ricardo's principal healing Spiritual guides are the Hathors and Buddha Kuan Yin who assists his distance healing work and mission. Other ascended healing masters also are at hand assisting during the distance healing session. Divine spiritual (God's) energy or *Tian qi – Divine Love –* through the higher soul is directed by a spiritual healer to heal a patient's disease at a distance.

The development of the Buddha nature can be accelerated by practicing the five virtues, doing service, having proper relationships with other people and with Mother Nature, and through regular practice of meditation.

A teacher named Annie Besant lived about a hundred years ago. She practiced loving-kindness by checking out the newspapers for people who had problems and needed help. Using her yogic powers, she blessed them so they would have a better life. If you are a healer, you can do the same thing by looking for people with problems and doing distant healing on them. - Master Choa Kok Sui

Quotes by Zen Master Kaneko Shoseki

"If the Absolute exists for us at all it must in some way be experienced by us as evident Reality, just as material objects are perceived by our senses. And for this there is only one way – to make a clean sweep of "scientific thinking" and to let the mind root itself in our innermost being. Whatever is presented to the merely outward I, not permeated by Being, is of only relative certainty.

True knowledge of the Absolute becomes possible only when its existence is experienced not merely as a theoretical necessity, but when it is felt personally within our innermost being. This Something so experienced is what I call the unquestionable creative rhythm of the life force, or the fundamental law of God which rules the whole world, and also that which gives us the highest standard of value by which to measure all our experiences. Only by this personal assurance can we free ourselves from the sins and delusions hidden in our bodies and minds and so become citizens of the Kingdom of Heaven. Philosophers, theologians, artists and moralists, generally speaking, attempt to find truth but until they have grasped that Something in personal experience their efforts will never cease to be a groping in the dark and will produce results of only superficial worth.

Original truth reveals itself only when one gives up all preconceived ideas. No suppositions, no theoretical thinking, no ideal concepts are helpful. All these will only confuse the soul in pursuit of an ever elusive Being and in the end he will have to confess with a sigh that all his striving has been meaningless and vain and that he would do better to live happily in modest ignorance than to be burdened with a really useless load of much-knowing. But all this is a fore-doomed tragedy which will never end until we know how to eradicate the roots of "Original Sin" by deep practice. In my opinion the Primordial is the essence or ground of the whole man, and the ordinary ego with its greed for so called objective knowledge is only the superstructure."

"The Primordial although it is in-dwelling in man's deepest being does not in any way belong to him for it is universal and only loaned to him by the highest Being. Therefore our minds and bodies and our very lives, through the Primordial Life Force, are dependent on the Absolute. We owe our whole existence never to ourselves but always to the Absolute. We ourselves are nothing; as nothing we belong to the Absolute."

"The living recognition of our absolute dependence on the highest Being is the perfect phenomenon of ultimate self-awareness. In the beginning man lost his Paradise through becoming conscious of himself. He can regain it only by achieving self-consciousness anew." – Kaneko Shoseki: *Nature and Origin of Man*

THE FIVE AGREEMENTS, A practical Guide to Self-Mastery

BE IMPECCABLE WITH YOUR WORD

Speak with integrity. Say only what you mean. Avoid using the word to speak against yourself or to gossip about others. Use the power of your word in the direction of truth and love.

DON'T TAKE ANYTHING PERSONALLY

Nothing others do is because of you. What others say and do is a projection of their own reality, their own dream. When you are immune to the opinions and actions of others, you won't be the victim of needless suffering.

DON'T MAKE ASSUMPTIONS

Find the courage to ask questions and to express what you really want. Communicate with others as clearly as you can to avoid misunderstandings, sadness, and drama. With just this one agreement, you can completely transform your life.

ALWAYS DO YOUR BEST

Your best is going to change from moment to moment; it will be different when you are healthy as opposed to sick. Under any circumstances, simply do your best, and you will avoid self-judgement, self-abuse, and regret.

BE SKEPTICAL, BUT LEARN TO LISTEN

Don't believe yourself or anybody else. Use the power of doubt to question everything you hear: Is it really the truth? Listen to the intent behind words, and you will understand the real message.

Source: The Fifth Agreement by Don Miguel Ruiz and Don Jose Ruiz, 2010.
www.miguelruiz.com

Hathor image carved in temple

Awakening the Sacred Space of the Heart Quotations

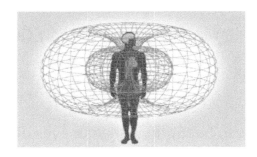

"The heart's electromagnetic field – by far the most powerful rhythmic field produced by the human body – not only envelops every cell of the body but also extends out in all directions into the space around us. The cardiac field can be measured several feet away from the body by sensitive devices. Research conducted at IHM suggests that the heart's field is an important carrier of information." – Institute HeartMath

"It is the heart that contains the original instructions of Life, and when the heart is again in control of a person's life, Life responds with joy and power.

When the Merkaba is directly connected to the Sacred Space of the Heart, that person's life becomes interconnected to all life everywhere and moves into higher consciousness naturally.

Learn to take your consciousness from the polarity of the brain into the unity of the heart and create a living organic Merkaba field aligned with Mother Earth and her coming changes. Live, create and heal from this place and experience the transformation!" – *Drunvalo Melchizedek*

If someone should say to you,
"In the fortified city of the imperishable,
our body, there is a lotus,
and in this lotus a tiny space:
what does it contain that one
should desire to know it?"

You must reply:
"As vast as this space without
is the tiny space within your heart:
heaven and earth are found in it,
fire and air, sun and moon,
lightning and the constellations,
whatever belongs to you here below
and all that doesn't,
all this is gathered in that tiny space
within your heart." – Chandogya Upanishad 8.1.2-3

NOTE by Ricardo B Serrano: *Awakening the Sacred Space of the Heart* is made possible through the practice of the *Ka (Merkaba) Meditation Procedure,* the *Omkabah Heart Lightbody Activation, Distance Healing Technique, Qigong,* and *Sun gazing.*

When We Created the World

It was lonely being the only One
And so I made two.
And then there was you.

You were so beautiful with your eyes of innocence
But I loved you from afar and yet so very near
And I loved you in ways you could not comprehend.

You didn't know I was watching through the eyes
of every person you met,
nor could you hear my voice in the wind.

You thought that the Earth was just dirt and rocks,
You didn't realize it was my body.

When you slept , we would meet in your heart
And make love with our spirits as One.
We would birth new worlds with such passion.

But when you were awake , you remembered nothing.

You thought it was just another dream.
It was just another day alone.

But in your heart I await you, my love, forever.
For the truth of our love and Oneness will always be.
Our love is the Matrix of All That Is.

Remember Sweet One,
In your heart I will always await thee
In the place that is small.

- Drunvalo Melchizedek, *Living in the Heart*

EPILOGUE

I am grateful to my spiritual guide the Hathors, *Masters of Sound and Love*, for their guidance and support during the writing and completion of this book. In the first place, they inspired me to start this book project to assist myself in handling my own fears and anger which have consistently bothered me for sometime before. Upon completing this book I am grateful for its healing and spiritual effects. You can stabilize chaotic emotions such as fear and anger and offer others an inner way out from these stressful emotions that keep affecting their health and peace of mind. The philosophy of this book especially with the other three books is a *pantheistic* perspective – *situated in the heart of that supreme energy of God Consciousness.* I have the complete energy-based how-to tools which allow you to master your emotions, heal yourself and others, and awaken spiritually in the process.

"This world is nothing but the blissful energy of the all-pervading consciousness of Lord Shiva. God and the individual are one, to realize this is the essence of Shaivism." - Swami Lakshmanjoo

The foundational basis of emotional mastery, healing and spiritual awakening is the activation and development of your *Sahhu* or lightbody with *awareness of being or presence in the gap* through toning (chanting the Four Sacred Elements mantras), the use of crystal bowls, crystals, Ka or lightbody meditation, *opening one's heart to unconditional love*, and distance healing others. By building the *Sahhu* (*golden lightbody*) and practicing *meditation on the gap or stillness*, one becomes aware of the Divine Presence not only within one's Self; one also becomes aware of the pervasive Divine presence.

According to Eckhart Tolle's How to Experience Total Freedom, "Access the power of Now. That is the key. The power of Now is none other than the power of your presence, your consciousness liberated from thought forms. So deal with the past on the level of the present. The more attention you give to the past, the more you energize it, and the more likely you are to make a "self" out of it.

Don't misunderstand: Attention is essential, but not to the past as past. Give attention to the present; give attention to your behaviour, to your reactions, moods, thoughts, emotions, fears, and desires as they occur in the present. There's the past in you. If you can be present enough to watch all those things, not critically or analytically but nonjudgmentally, then you are dealing with the past and dissolving it through the power of your presence – inner space or awareness.
You cannot find yourself by going into the past. You find yourself by coming into the present."

There are other portals for spiritual empowerment that can be used to access the Unmanifested Source other than being intensely present, and these are: getting in touch with the energy field of your lightbody, disidentify from the mind, surrender to what is, paying attention in the gap between sound and silence, and the gap between object and space, and paying attention in the gap between inbreath and outbreath.

According to Swami Lakshmanjoo, "According to the theory of Shaivism, you are Shiva, and you will eventually come to the conclusion that you are Shiva. And yet, you are not actually Shiva, because you have not achieved that state.

Even though you have not actually realized that you are Shiva, it is not a mistake to think that you are Shiva. You should go on thinking that you are Shiva. You should always elevate yourself with the thought that you are Lord Shiva – but do not boast of this. If you tell someone that you are Shiva it means that you are not Lord Shiva. You must actually understand that if you are Lord Shiva, then this whole creation is all a joke, an expression of your play.

One might ask, "How do you know whether or not you are fooling yourself thinking that you are Shiva, or whether you really are Lord Shiva? How do you know?" The answer is that you will come to know yourself because you will be blissful, you will always be blissful. When you are in that state and when something bad happens to you, you will not get worried; and when something good happens to you, you will not get excited. While experiencing pain you will be peaceful.

You must come to know and see in yourself situated in this way. If you are not situated in this way and boast, saying, "I am Lord Shiva, I am Lord Shiva," you will be slapped and made to understand that you are not Lord Shiva.

To actually know who you are is a big problem. You have to find out yourself where you are situated. It happens by the grace of Lord Shiva, or by the grace of a master, or by the grace of the *sastras* (scriptures).

The nature of the universe is the existence of Lord Shiva. Lord Shiva's existence is naturally everyone's nature. Lord Shiva is found in rocks; Lord Shiva is found everywhere. Lord Shiva is even found in the absence of Lord Shiva. Even there He is not absent, He is existing.

There He resides, alone in His kingdom. No one else is found there."

The necessary principles behind the development of your Ka or lightbody are explained together with the awareness and preliminary knowledge about your pranic tube, Ka of the Sun, heart of Mother Earth, Tube Torus, your sacred space of your heart's unconditional love, your Merkaba or lightbody, *Meditation on the Gap,* and *being present*. The books that are invaluable in the research of this book are *Hathor Material* by Tom Kenyon and Virginia Essene, *Son of the Sun* by Savitri Devi, *Emerald Tablets of Thoth the Atlantean* by Doreal, *Healing Tones of Crystal Bowls* by Renee Brodie, *Vibrational Medicine* by Dr. Richard Gerber, *Living in the Heart* by Drunvalo Melchizedek, Swami Lakshmanjoo's *Shiva Sutras* and *Self Realization in Kashmir Shaivism,* Eckhart Tolle's *Power of Now,* and other books in the Reference Books page. I'm very grateful and thankful to these authors for their contribution to the research of this book.

Additional important adjuncts such as the Toltec wisdom of Dr. Miguel Ruiz - the *Five Agreements for Self-Mastery,* and additional information on the effect of emotional stress to health presented by Dr. Candace Pert's *Molecules of Emotion*, and Dr. Nelie Johnson's *You Hold the Keys to Your Healing* are included.

To complement the *Ka or Merkaba Meditation Procedure*, I would also recommend that you learn meditation and Qigong covered in my other three books *Meditation and Qigong Mastery, Return to Oneness with the Tao*, and *Return to Oneness with Spirit through Pan Gu Shen Gong*.

May you regularly practice the *Ka (Merkaba) Meditation, Distance Healing, Sun gazing,* and other practices elaborated in this book. May you also view *Omkabah Heart Lightbody Activation* and *Maitreya (Shiva) Shen Gong* videos, and also visit my Vancouver Qigong Mastery at qigongmastery.ca for regular updates, and attend my meditation / Qigong workshops. The following *Ka*-building article "*Budwig Diet for Cancer and Chronic Diseases*" will complete your healing nutritionally. The article "*Sahhu* or *Immortal Golden Lightbody and Its Soul Powers*" which is the goal of most schools of meditation, Qi-healing and Qigong for Self-realization will be elaborated together with *Sun Yoga and Its Healing and Enlightenment Aspects* and *Enlightenment Qigong Forms for Returning to Oneness*.

May you reach the goal of meditation and Qigong – Self-realization through your *Sahhu* or *immortal golden lightbody.*

Ricardo B Serrano, R.Ac.
Holographic Sound Healing Facilitator

Budwig Diet for Cancer and Chronic Diseases

"The essential fatty acids are at the core of the answer to the cancer problem."
– Dr Robert Willner, MD, PhD., The Cancer Solution

INTRODUCTORY NOTE by Ricardo B Serrano, R.Ac.: For best healing results of chronic diseases such as cancer, heart disease, stroke, arthritis, and other diseases, the simple Diet of Dr. Johanna Budwig – cottage cheese and Flaxseed oil combined with flax seeds – builds the *Ka pranic body, Qi life-force* and *Jing* (essence), and can be integrated with meditation, Qigong, and other Oriental medical treatments.

The two unsaturated fatty acids have 3 high-energy double bonds (pi-electrons). These fatty acids affect the membranes of cells and are believed to affect oxygen transport and assimilation. Budwig's concept was that the omega-3 and omega-6 fatty acids act to repair damaged cell walls and affect chemical communication of cancer cells to the point where they normalize.

Flaxseed oil (cold-pressed, unprocessed) and low fat cottage cheese are the mainstay of Budwig's cancer diet (also used for heart disease) (cottage cheese has actually become to be used as a more readily-available substitute for the quark cheese which Johanna Budwig had used in her original work).

In addition to the above components, the Budwig diet advocates the consumption of organic vegetable juices (most prominently carrot juice) and polyphenols such as resveratrol (found in red wine). The diet bans consumption of animal and hydrogenated fats, foods high in preservatives, meats, and especially sugar. She advocated the consumption of whole foods which contain antioxidants in their natural form.

Budwig claimed this diet would cure or prevent many forms of cancers, particularly breast and prostate cancer, and a long list of other degenerative disease including cardiovascular diseases and skin diseases.

FOOTNOTE: *Jing* is the first Treasure and is translated as "Regenerative Essence," or simply as "Essence." *Jing* is the refined energy of the body. It provides the foundation for all activity and is said to be the "root" of our vitality. *Jing* is the primal energy of life. It is closely associated with our genetic potential, and is associated with the aging process. *Jing* is stored energy and provides the reserves required to adapt to all the various stresses encountered in life. Since *Jing* is concentrated energy, it manifests materially. *Jing* also is said to control a number of primary human functions: the reproductive organs and their various substances and functions; the power and clarity of the mind; and the integrity of one's physical structure. *Jing*, which is a blend of Yin and Yang energy, is said to be stored in the "Kidney." *Jing* is generally associated these days with the hormones of the reproductive and adrenal glands, and *Jing* is the vital essence concentrated in the sperm and ova.

When *Jing* is strong, vitality and youthfulness remain. Strong *Jing* energy in the Kidneys, so the Chinese say, will lead to a long and vigorous life, while a loss of *Jing* will result in physical and mental degeneration and a shortening of one's life. *Jing* is essential to life and when it runs low our life force is severely diminished and thus we lose all power to adapt. The quantity of Essence determines both our life span and the ultimate vitality of our life. *Jing* is burned up in the body by life itself, but most especially by chronic and acute stress and excessive behavior, including overwork, excessive emotionalism, substance abuse, chronic pain or illness, and marital excess (especially in men). Excessive menstrual patterns, pregnancy and childbirth can result in a dramatic drain on the *Jing* of a woman, especially in middle aged women. When *Jing* is depleted below a level required to survive, we die. Eventually everyone runs out of *Jing* and thus everyone dies (at least physically).

Dr Budwig, in her book, *Flax Oil As A True Aid Against Arthritis, Heart Infarction, Cancer And Other Diseases* also brought up the relationship between the Fats Syndrome, Electrons, Photons, and Solar Energy provided by the Sun.

She pointed out that the sun is an inexhaustible source of energy and an element of life that affects the vital functions of the body. This, in part, is due to the photons in sunlight which are the purest form of energy, the purest wave, and in continual movement. Dr Budwig states, "electrons are already a constituent of matter, even though they are also in continual movement and that electrons love photons, attracting each other due to their magnetic fields. There is nothing else on earth with a higher concentration of photons of the sun's energy than man. This concentration of the sun's energy – very much an iso-energetic point for humans, with their eminently suitable wave lengths – is improved when we eat food which has electrons which in turn attract the electro-magnetic waves of sun beams, of photons.

A high amount of these electrons which are on the wave length of the sun's energy, are to be found, for example, in seed oils. Scientifically, these oils are even known as electron–rich essential highly unsaturated fats. But, when people began to treat fats to make them keep longer, no one stopped to consider the consequences of this, for the existence and higher development of the human race. These vitally important amounts of electrons, with their continual movement and wonderful reaction of light were destroyed."

Dr Budwig found when she treated patients and had them lie in the sun she noticed they started feeling much better and became rejuvenated. She referred to the sun as having a stimulating effect on the secretions of the liver, gall bladder, pancreas, bladder and salivary glands. Dr Budwig also stated "Matter always has its own vibration, and so, of course, does the living body. The absorption of energy must correspond to one's own wave length." It appears apparently that sunlight is absolutely essential for the stimulation effect of the vital functions of the mind and body, contributing to the factors which allow the body to heal itself.

Dr Budwig mentioned that doctors tell patients and cancer patients to avoid the sun as they can't tolerate it and that is correct. She says once these patients start on her oil-protein nutritional advice for two or three days which means they have been getting sufficient amounts of essential fats, they can then tolerate the sun very well. She said the patients then tell her how much better they feel as their vitality and vigor is re-stimulated.

The last of the points mentioned by Dr Budwig and maybe the most important, is the electrons in our food serve as the resonance system for the sun's energy and are truly the element of life. Man acts as an antenna for the sun. The interplay between the photons in the sunbeams and the electrons in the seed oils and our foods, governs all the vital functions of the body.

This has to be one of the greatest discoveries ever made as this combination promotes healing in the body of chronic and terminal diseases. In her book Dr Budwig states "Various highly trained and educated individuals are dismayed and irritated by the fact that serious medical conditions can be cured by cottage cheese and flaxseed oil."

The mixing of the oil and cottage cheese allows for the chemical reaction to take place between the sulfur protein in the cottage cheese and the oil, which makes the oil water soluble for easy absorption into your cells.

The Budwig Protocol

Only use Flax Oil from the refrigerated section of your health food store. Never use capsules, flakes or flax oil from the shelves. It must be refrigerated and check the expiration date to make sure it has not expired. I would not use High Lignan Flax Oil because the taste is not clean and you can not tell if it is rancid. They have left the husk from the processing of the seeds in the bottom of the bottle, leaving less product. You want good clean tasting oil and no flavoring added as some oils are doing.

The mixing ratio is two tablespoons of cottage cheese to one tablespoon of oil. Mix only the amount you are consuming at one time so it is mixed fresh each and every time. One example would be to mix (4) tablespoons of cottage cheese to (2) tablespoons of flax oil, consumed twice daily or more depending on the severity of the health condition, one is attempting to address. One should probably start slowly with the oil, maybe just once a day and work their way up letting the body adjust to the protocol. The oil and the cottage cheese must be thoroughly mixed at a low speed, using an Immersion Blender, blending until a creamy texture with no standing oil is achieved.

The mixture should then be immediately consumed. Do not add anything to the mixture until after it is mixed!!

We have always recommended using the immersion [stick or wand like] mixer for the Flax Seed Oil and Cottage Cheese.

One may want to consider sprinkling a tablespoon or two of freshly ground flax seed over top of the freshly mixed flax oil and cottage cheese mixture. Mix this in by hand. This super charges the protocol. Do not buy pre-ground flax seed as the flax seed goes rancid 15 minutes after grinding. Brown or Golden whole flaxseed is available at the health food stores and either will work. You may grind up the fresh flax seed with a small coffee grinder. Store the seeds in the refrigerator and grind fresh each time.

You may also stir in with a spoon 2-3 tablespoons of organic low fat milk for a creamer mixture. This can be mixed in by hand after the initial blending. The mixture can be flavored differently every day by adding nuts, preferably organic such as pecans, almonds or walnuts (not peanuts), banana, organic cocoa, organic shredded coconut, pineapple (fresh), blueberries, raspberries, cinnamon, or (freshly) squeezed fruit juice. It's usually best to place the fresh fruit on top of the completed mixture and enjoy as its own meal. Try your best to obtain organic fruit when possible. Many times this can be found frozen when not in season.

Dr Budwig pointed out that people who are suffering from Chronic or Terminal disease should work themselves up to consuming 4 - 8 Tbsp of the oil daily. Usually the higher limits 6 - 8 Tbsp were for people with cancer. She stated, people with Liver or Pancreatic Cancer etc, may have to work up very slowly with the oil and possibly only start with 1 teaspoon at a time giving their body time to adjust. Dr Budwig pointed out that cancer patients once starting the protocol and getting it under control must continue with a maintenance dose to prevent reoccurrence. A maintenance dose is considered (1) Tbsp of the oil per one hundred pounds of body weight. The Budwig Diet takes time to work and in the event of cancer, tumors, etc may take 3-6 months to see results. Many other health issues may respond much faster.

If you are Lactose Intolerant you may want to try the following. Since commercial milk is pasteurized, beneficial bacteria and enzymes in the milk and dairy products are destroyed. This has led to a number of people having difficulty in tolerating quark or cottage cheese.

Dairy is an important component in Dr. Budwig's Oil-Protein Diet. Because good substitutes are hard to find, it is worthwhile for those who are lactose intolerant to try different ways of tolerating dairy.

Some possibilities (in no particular order):
Use raw milk and raw milk products if you can get them.
Use goat's milk instead of cow's milk products.
Take the enzyme Lactase with quark or cottage cheese.
Try Nancy's Cottage Cheese which is made with lactic cultures.

Make yogurt quark

Make kefir quark (straining kefir to get a cream cheese consistency)

Get kefir grains, make kefir, remove grains, and strain through fine muslin cloth.

To learn more, do a Google search for "kefir" it will get you many hits.

"Kefir cottage cheese (or quark) is most certainly our solution for lactose intolerant people. It works like a charm."

If one does not wish to make kefir, it can be purchased from the health food store in the refrigerated section. Organic Kefir comes in a liquid and the oil may be stirred into the kefir and consumed. It tastes very good. Make sure the oil is totally dissolved into the kefir before consuming. You may want to check with the health food store and see if they have a kefir cheese similar to cottage cheese which should work, as long as the flax oil blends in and does not float back to the top.

In the case of a person with a feeding tube one could mix flax oil into the organic kefir by hand as mentioned above. Then pour into the feeding tube. Again, this can be done using ¼ cup kefir to 1 tablespoon of the flax oil and given through out the day at different times. You may be able to use even a little more oil with the ¼ cup kefir. One may have to play with the mixture to get the desired results. Make sure there is no oil floating on top of the kefir before pouring into the feeding tube.

It has been mentioned in several articles that once a chronic or terminal disease has been brought under control or into remission the amount of flax oil may be reduced to (1) tablespoon per hundred lbs. of body weight for maintenance. To prevent reoccurrence of the cancer one should stay on the maintenance dose.

If yogurt is used in place of the cottage cheese it will require 3 times more yogurt to be consumed than cottage cheese as it lacks the protein density of cottage cheese. Even then, this may not be as effective. There is some question, as Dr Budwig never addressed this issue. The yogurt will have to be (live cultures, not the kind in the supermarket). An example of using the yogurt would be ¾ cup of yogurt to 1 tablespoon of flax oil.

The following items listed below should be avoided on this diet.
(The reason one needs to exclude these items from his / her diet is that they interfere with the diet by lowering the voltage field in the cells.)

Sugar
All animal fats (hydrogenated)
All meats especially pork, seafood with hard shell
Margarine
Butter
Salad dressing oils- exception extra virgin olive oil and balsamic vinegar or lemon
Foods high in Preservatives

Dr Budwig Diet Plan

To start the diet, it helps to have 3 appliances. One is a coffee bean grinder to grind the whole brown flaxseeds sold in health food stores or online. In Dr Budwig's protocol she used 2 to 3 tablespoons daily of the ground up flax seed. The flax seeds should be ground and used immediately. They must be consumed within 15 minutes of grinding or considered rancid. They can be used in cereals, oatmeal, shakes etc.

The 2nd appliance is an immersion hand-held mixer, a somewhat stick-shaped mixer, to blend the flaxseed oil [FO] and the cottage cheese [CC] together so that they become one food, making the oil water-soluble and more absorbable to the cells of the body.

The 3rd appliance needed is a vegetable juicer. A masticating-type may give a more healthful juice than a centrifugal type. Purchasing a vegetable juicer is absolutely essential.

Patients with liver, gallbladder or pancreatic cancer, may need to start with a lesser amount of the oil and build up slowly to Dr Budwig's recommended dosage.

THE RECOMMENDED DIET

The diet which is slowly being recognized by all medical authorities as a cancer preventive stresses the intake of:

FRESH FRUITS.................. 3 to 4 MEDIUM SIZE PORTIONS DAILY.

FRESH VEGETABLES............ 4 to 6 CUPS (SEVERAL TABLESPOONS OF LINSEEDS AND/OR 1 TO 2 TABLESPOONS OF THE OIL CAN BE USED IN THE SALAD DRESSING OR ON THE VEGETABLES, BE SURE TO INCLUDE CABBAGE, BROCCOLI, AND MAITAKE MUSHROOMS.

UNPROCESSED WHOLE GRAIN BREADS AND CEREALS..................... 3 to 4 CUPS OR PORTIONS.

FRESH FISH (PREFERABLY COLD WATER VARIETY).......................... 4 to 8 oz. An excellent source of the omega-3 fatty acids is rainbow trout.

FRESH MEAT - BRED WITHOUT HORMONES, FAT-PRODUCING DIETS, OR FEED THAT HAS BEEN GROWN WITH PESTICIDES OR ANTIBIOTICS.... 3oz.

TWO TO THREE TIMES A WEEK.

LIQUIDS - BOTTLED WATER. IF POSSIBLE IT SHOULD BE PURIFIED BY REVERSE OSMOSIS, DISTILLATION AND OZONATION. THERE ARE MANY INDIVIDUALS WHO HAVE DIFFICULTY WITH DRINKING THE EIGHT GLASSES A DAY THAT IS RECOMMENDED. SUGGESTION: PLACE ONE GLASS OF YOUR FAVORITE JUICE IN A LITER OR QUART BOTTLE AND FILL THE REMAINDER WITH WATER. IT IS REFRESHING. (*I use **alkaline kangen water** for best results*).

DON'T FORGET -

HERBAL TEAS, ESSAIC FORMULA, CHAPARRAL, ETC.

FRESH FRUIT JUICES (CITRUS FRUITS SHOULD NOT BE TAKEN WITHIN SEVERAL HOURS OF THE LINSEED OIL - COTTAGE CHEESE PORTIONS)

CAUTION: REMEMBER THAT EATING ANY PROCESSED OILS WILL COUNTERACT EVERYTHING YOU ARE TRYING TO DO. THEY ARE POISON, AS ARE ALL FRIED FOODS. ELIMINATE AS MUCH SUGAR AS POSSIBLE FROM THE DIET. REMEMBER THAT HONEY (NOT ROYAL JELLY) IS PRIMARILY SUGAR. PREPARED FOODS MUST BE DEVOID OF ALL ARTIFICIAL PRESERVATIVES OR CHEMICAL ADDITIVES. ARTIFICIAL SWEETENERS ARE ABSOLUTELY FORBIDDEN! IF GOD DIDN'T MAKE IT OR YOU CAN'T PRONOUNCE IT – DON'T EAT IT!

HELPFUL HINTS;

The first time I tried linseed oil on a salad, I was pleasantly surprised. I had expected it to taste strange or unusual. It didn't - IT TASTED GREAT! The mixture with the low fat cottage cheese was even more exciting than I anticipated. I actually looked forward to eating a slice of the multi-grain bread covered with a thick layer of the mixture. I do realize that you cannot argue taste, and that taste varies tremendously. With that In mind, I am providing a whole list of ingredients and suggestions for ways of making the Budwig "formula" a delight for your palate.

BREAKFAST:

Fruit Juice

Cereal - ground linseeds, whole grains, nuts, raisins, chopped fresh fruits, linseed oil low-fat cottage cheese, 1/3 to 1/2 cup low-fat milk, and honey. Mixed well in a blender.

Eggs - Blend 2 eggs with 1 teaspoon of linseed oil and 1 tablespoon low-fat cottage cheese. Add chopped tomato, onions, green pepper, herbs and spices. Slowly bake or broil.

"Coffee" - Made from roasted cereals.

LUNCH or DINNER:

Salad - Any desired mixture of greens, vegetables, or fruits.

Dressings: Low-fat cottage cheese and linseed oil mixture, then add the ingredients for the following dressings:

Honey Mustard: 1 tsp. honey and 1/2 tsp. of Dijon mustard

Creamy Italian: Vinegar, herbs (Italian); then for taste variation add any combination of spices, mustard, raw egg, garlic, onion powder, crushed anchovies.

Green Goddess: Minced spinach, cucumber, parsley, lemon and dill.

Mexican: Minced chile, red peppers, tomato, onion, herbs and spices.

Fruit: Honey, crushed nuts, poppy seeds and linseeds and a touch of cinnamon, lemon and/or mustard, if desired.

SOUPS:

Gazpacho Soup: Dilute (basic mixture) with low-fat milk and add: tomatos, garlic, cucumber, onions, herbs and spices-blend well and chill.

Bean Soups: Prepare your favorite soup in the usual way and add the Budwig mix to it.

Other Soups: Tomato and onion soups can be made as usual and the Budwig mix added.

COOKED VEGETABLES: Lightly steam, and then coat with linseed oil and spices. Honey and oil are great for corn and sweet potato. Baked potato is good with mix, oil alone, or with onions, parsley, etc.

Desert: The basic mixture plus cut-up peaches, berries, flavoring, nuts, cinnamon, cloves, nutmeg, honey, or your personal creativeness.

IF YOU HAVE CANCER:
IT IS IMPERATIVE THAT YOU FOLLOW THE DIET EXACTLY - NO CHEATING IS ALLOWED! DR. BUDWIG PLACED GREAT STRESS ON FOLLOWING THE DIET EXACTLY. HER MANY YEARS OF EXPERIENCE HAVE CONVINCED HER THAT FAILURES DO NOT OCCUR EXCEPT WHEN THE PATIENT IS LAX WITH HER TREATMENT. USE THE LINSEED OIL MORE FREQUENTLY IN MEALS AND SNACKS.

WRAPPING LINSEED OIL SOAKED CLOTHS ON TO THE PART OF THE BODY THAT IS EFFECTED WITH CANCER IS VERY HELPFUL. FOR EXAMPLE, IF YOU HAVE A LIVER CANCER, WRAP THE WAIST. IF IT IS THE LUNGS, WRAP THE CHEST. IF IT IS THE BRAIN, WRAP THE HEAD AND NECK, AND SO ON. THIS IS BEST ACCOMPLISHED DURING THE NIGHT AND WHENEVER THE OPPORTUNITY ALLOWS. THE OIL CAN BE MIXED WITH ROSE WATER TO ADD AN AESTHETIC TOUCH. COLD PRESSED AND UNPROCESSED WALNUT, PUMPKIN AND SOYBEAN OIL CAN BE USED IN ADDITION TO LINSEED OIL FOR VARIETY.

SUNSHINE - Sun on the skin is very healthful for vitamin D & other benefits but avoid burning.

EXERCISE; INDIVIDUALIZE IT ACCORDING TO YOUR STRENGTH NEVER OVER DO IT. Dr. Budwig did not push the idea of exercise, she felt that one needs rest to heal. So, take caution. [For those who can exercise, besides walking, a rebounder (a small, round trampoline) is beneficial for the lymph system, heart & circulation. RELAXATION IN THE SUN IF POSSIBLE to relieve stress is healing - nature, music, chat, laughter.[On days when you cannot be in the sun, high-quality cold-pressed cod liver oil offers vitamin D & other benefits]

DR BUDWIG STRESSED THAT IT IS VERY IMPORTANT TO AVOID UNHEALTHY FOODS & SUBSTANCES such as hydrogenated fats, animal fats, sugar, white flour, preservatives, chemicals and processed foods. Avoid leftovers – food should be prepared fresh and eaten soon after preparation to get the health-giving electrons & enzymes – within 15-20 minutes. At least 3x a day drink a warm liquid, such as green or herbal teas, sweeten only with raw honey. Keep a food diary. Avoid stress and anxiety; take time to relax & enjoy each day. Listen to beautiful music, laugh, do deep breathing, connect with nature, and spend time with people you like. Dr Budwig spoke about the damaging effects of stress.

Also, she did not include supplements or drugs in her protocol. Some supplements, especially high amounts of antioxidants, can interfere with how well the diet works, as can some drugs.

Dr Budwig in her protocol also used Eldi R Oils and Oil packs to help in the healing process of chronic and terminal diseases. Dr Budwig created the Eldi Oils (Electron Differentiation oils) through exact spectroscopic measurements via the absorption of light in different oils. The Eldi Oils have a favorable 'retuning' effect on the metabolism for people who are ill. The 'retuning' effect relates to the creation of oxygen and energy within the system. The sun's energy resonates with the electronic energy created by the flax oil and cottage cheese combination, and the Eldi oils do exactly the same when applied topically to the skin or as a rectal enema. When applying in a rectal enema it appeared she used ½ cup to 1 cup of the oils daily. It appears a person would hold the oil for about 15-20 minutes before release. I guess common sense will have to prevail. If Eldi oils are not available one can use Flax Oil.

The following protocol on how Dr Budwig used Eldi Oil R was sent to me from Germany by Wolfgang Bloching. The Eldi Oil R is essential in this healing protocol. Wolfgang also advised that Dr Budwig when necessary used the Eldi Oil R in (Rectal Enemas). This was used for the very sick. The oils can be purchased from Wolfgang by contacting him at the following e-mail address: Wolfgang.Bloching@t-online.de

Dr. J. Budwig Eldi Oel R (Eldi Oil R): Application

Two times a day, i.e. morning and evening, rub Eldi Oil R into the skin over the whole body, a bit more intensively on the shoulders (armpits), breast and groin (where the lymphatic vessels are) and also on the problem areas, like for instance the breast, stomach, liver, etc. Leave the oil on the skin for about 15-20 minutes. Then take a warm shower without soap. Then follow up with another shower, this time using a mild soap. Then rest for 15-20 minutes. The purpose of the shower, after the body has been oiled and the Eldi Oil has penetrated the skin, is that the warm water opens the pores so that the oil can penetrate a bit deeper into the skin. The second shower, this time with soap, is for skin surface cleaning so that clothes and linen will not become soiled too much.

Always use the Eldi Oil R in connection with the Oil-Protein Diet (Budwig Diet) and do this consistently, even if it seems difficult at times. The Oil-Protein Diet together with Eldi Oil is a helpful method to improve problems and illnesses long term. The Eldi Oils in small bottles with 95 ml content are all perfumed and contain, like Eldi Oil R, only highly unsaturated fatty acids, but they are too expensive to be used for the whole body. They are meant to be used this way for example:
Eldi Oel photo activ (photo active) only for the face.
Eldi Oel Rose for a woman's body (rose oil).
Eldi Oel herb neu (tart new) for a man's body (tart scent).
Eldi Oel H-activ (H-active) only for the breast region (heart) etc.

Eldi Oel balsamicum Salbei (balsamic sage) is only for oil packs. Take pure cotton 100% or a cotton cloth. Cut these to size for the body part, for example the knee. Soak the cotton, place on the knee, cover the cotton with a plastic sheet and wrap it all with an elastic bandage. Leave it on for the night. Remove it in the morning and wash the knee. Repeat it in the evening and do this for weeks. You can also use Eldi Oil R for these local applications. The oil pack is only suited for local problems (no metastases).

Dr. Johanna Budwig's Books:

1. Flax Oil As A True Aid Against Arthritis, Heart Infarction, Cancer And Other Diseases
2. The Oil Protein Diet Cook Book
3. Cancer: The Problem and Solution

Fats that Kill –Trans-fatty acid (margarine, fried junk foods and shortening)

Excerpts from Dr. Robert E. Willner's *The Cancer Solution*

"Numerous, independent clinical studies published in major medical journals world-wide confirm Dr. Budwig's findings ... Over 40 years ago Dr Budwig presented clear and convincing evidence, which has been confirmed by hundreds of other related scientific research papers since, that the *essential fatty acids were at the core of the answer to the cancer problem* ... You will come to your own conclusions as to why this simple effective prevention and therapy has not only been ignored – it has been suppressed!"
– Dr Robert Willner, M.D., Ph.D. (The Cancer Solution)

According to the Budwig Diet by Dr. Robert Willner, "Six time nobel award nominated doctor says this essential nutrient combination actually prevents and cures cancer!

A top European cancer research scientist, Dr Johanna Budwig, has discovered a totally natural formula that not only protects against the development of cancer but people all over the world who have been diagnosed with incurable cancer and sent home to die have actually been cured and now lead normal healthy lives.

After three decades of research Dr. Budwig, six-time nominee for the Nobel Award, found that the blood of seriously ill cancer patients was always, without exception, deficient in certain important essential ingredients which included substances called phosphatides and lipoproteins. (The blood of a healthy person always contains sufficient quantities of these essential ingredients. However, without these natural ingredients cancer cells grow wild and out of control.)

Blood analysis showed a strange greenish-yellow substance in place of the healthy red oxygen carrying hemoglobin that belongs there. This explained why cancer patients weaken and become anemic This startling discovery led Dr. Budwig to test her theory.

She found that when these natural ingredients where replaced over approximately a three month period, tumors gradually receded. The strange greenish elements in the blood were replaced with healthy red blood cells as the phosphatides and lipoproteins almost miraculously reappeared. Weakness and anemia disappeared and life energy was restored. Symptoms of cancer, liver dysfunction and diabetes were completely alleviated.

Dr. Budwig then discovered an all natural way for people to replace those essential ingredients their bodies so desperately needed in their daily diet. By simply eating a combination of just two natural and delicious foods not only can cancer be prevented but in case after case it was actually cured. (These two natural foods, organic flax seed oil & cottage cheese) must be eaten together to be effective since one triggers the properties of the other to be released.)

After more than 10 years of solid clinical application, Dr. Budwig's natural formula has proven successful where many orthodox remedies have failed. Dr. Budwig's formula has been used therapeutically in Europe for prevention of: Cancer! Arteriosclerosis, Strokes, Cardiac Infarction, Heartbeat (irregular), Liver (fatty degeneration), Lungs (reduces bronchial spasms), Intestines (regulates activity), Stomach Ulcers (normalizes gastric juices), Prostate (hypertopic), Arthritis (exerts a favorable influence), Eczema (assists all skin diseases), Old age (improves many common afflictions), Brain (strengthens activity), Immune Deficiency Syndromes (multiple sclerosis, auto-immune illnesses).

Thousands have flocked to hear Dr. Budwig lecture all over Europe. The many people Dr. Budwig's formula has helped testify to the benefits of her remarkable discovery. Following are a few examples: In one of my interviews with Dr. Budwig I was introduced to Siegried Ernst, M.D.. He is a rare and dedicated man who counts among his personal friends the current Pope as well as many other dignitaries.

Seventeen years ago Dr. Ernst had developed cancer for which he had major surgery requiring removal of his stomach. Two years later he had a recurrence of the cancer and was offered chemotherapy as the only available remedy. There was little hope for survival as virtually all individuals with recurrence of this type of cancer rarely last a year.

Dr. Ernst knew that chemotherapy was not only ineffective for his type of cancer but completaly destructive of the quality of life, so he refused.

He turned to Dr. Budwig and her formula for help. He religiously followed Dr. Budwig's formula and fifteen years later has not had any recurrence of cancer. As a matter of fact he seemed to me to be in perfect health and is tireless for a man in his late seventies.

Maria W. tells her story in her own words: "I was told by the most expert of doctors that I would have to be operated on to cut out the cancerous tumor that was causing a swelling under my eye. They explained that the size of the tumor was much greater inside and that there was very serious bone involvement. The malignancy was too far advanced to respond to radiation treatment. The doctors planned to remove considerable facial tissue and bone. I was afraid for my life, but being a young woman, couldn't bear the thought of such disfigurement.

When I heard about Dr. Budwig's natural formula, I was skeptical but desperate for help. After four months on this regimen, the swelling under my left eye completely disappeared. The doctors at the University hospital gave me many exhausting tests. One told me, 'If I didn't have your previous x-rays and medical history in front of me, I wouldn't believe that you ever had cancer. There is hardly any indication of a tumor remaining.' I never thought using Dr. Budwig's formula would be so successful. My whole family and I are very grateful."

An examination of Sandy A. revealed arachnoidal bleeding due to an inoperable brain tumor. The doctors informed Sandy that he was beyond medical help. At his expressed wish, Sandy was discharged from the hospital and sent home to die in peace.

A friend brought Dr. Budwig's formula to Sandy's attention. Sandy writes. "Since I went on the Budwig regimen, the paralysis is of my eyes, arms, and legs has receded daily. After only a short period of time, I was able to urinate normally. My health improved so rapidly that I was soon able to return to my work part-time. Shortly after that, I was again examined at the Research Center and my reflexes were completely normal. The Budwig diet saved my life! Ten years later, I was given a thorough examination at the Center as a follow-up. My incredible recovery has been written up In many medical journals and I have become what they call a 'text-book case,' and all because of Dr. Johanna Budwig's simple diet."

Seven years ago Timmy G. was diagnosed as having Hodgkins disease. The child was operated on and underwent 24 radiation treatments, plus additional experimental therapies that the experts hoped would be of some small help. When Timmy failed to respond favorably to these heroic measures, he was discharged as incurable, and given six months to live and sent home to die.

The desperate parents contacted specialists all over the world. A famous newspaper took up Timmy's cause and ran editorials pleading for someone to come forth who could offer hope for the life of a child. All the specialists who replied confirmed the cruel prognosis: There was no hope or help for Timmy. At this dark hour the miracle the family had prayed for happened! Timmy's mother told her story to the press:

"A friend sent me a printed piece about one of Dr. Budwig's speeches. This material gave us hope and I contacted Dr. Budwig.

In just five days, (on the Budwig regimen) Timmy's breathing became normal for the first lime In almost two years. From this day on, Timmy began to feel good again. He went back to school, started swimming and by winter he was doing craft work. Everyone who knows him says how well he looks." At age 18 Timmy is showing great promise in his university work. He knows he owes his life to Dr. Budwig and thanks her daily in his prayers.

One of the two foods in on Budwig's formula, cottage cheese, is available in nearly every grocery store in America. The other, pure organic linseed oil, however comes primarily from Europe and can only be found in certain health food stores throughout the United States.

By simply mixing these two delicious foods together and eating them you will be providing yourself and your family with the optimal preventive nutritional protection against cancer and other disease."

Quotations from other holistic doctors

"What she (Dr. Johanna Budwig) has demonstrated to my initial disbelief but lately, to my complete satisfaction in my practice is: CANCER IS EASILY CURABLE, the treatment is dietary/lifestyle, the response is immediate; the cancer cell is weak and vulnerable; the precise biochemical breakdown point was identified by her in 1951 and is specifically correctable, in vitro (test-tube) as well as in vivo (real)... " Dr. Dan C. Roehm M.D. FACP (Oncologist and former cardiologist) in 1990 http://www.oxytherapy.com/mail-archive/oct96/165.html

"Cancer patients suffer from a faulty metabolism caused by a malfunction in the lipid defense system. By repairing the lipid defense system the cancer cannot survive. Of course common chemo and radiation causes further harm to the lipid defense system – the very system that protects you from cancer! The folks who will READILY ADMIT that they don't understand the cancer mechanism will tell you with their next breath that cancer can be killed with poisons. So can you. Would you trust your car to a so-called mechanic who didn't understand what makes a car work properly? If not, why would you let someone who doesn't understand cancer "fix" your body? The average cancer docs don't know -- they admit it. That doesn't make them bad people, it just makes them unqualified to treat your condition if you have cancer. Don't let unqualified people poison you just because they don't know what else to do". – William Kelley Eidem, author "The Doctor Who Cures Cancer" (Dr Revici)

"I have the answer to cancer, but American doctors won't listen. They come here and observe my methods and are impressed. Then they want to make a special deal so they can take it home and make a lot of money. I won't do it, so I'm blackballed in every country." – Dr Budwig

"Nobody seemed to notice that a crime has been committed: It was the case of the missing nutrient. The nutrient was essential; it was a nutrient we human beings needed in order to stay healthy. It started to disappear from our diet about 75 years ago and now is almost gone. Only about 20% of the amount needed for human health and well-being remains. The nutrient is a fatty acid so important and so little understood that I call it "the nutritional missing link" ... Food grade linseed oil & fish oil are the best sources of this special fat – Omega 3 essential fatty acid – which modern food destroys." – Donald Rudin, M.D. (The Omega 3 Phenomenon)

In a 1994 study of 121 women with breast cancer, those in more advanced stages whose breast cancer had spread to their lymph nodes showed the lowest levels of omega-3 fatty acids in the breast tissue. After 31 months, the 20 women who had developed metastases had significantly lower levels of these EFAs (Essential fatty acids) than those who didn't. Another study out of Boston University using the same type of tissue profiles that were used in the breast cancer study demonstrated that patients with coronary artery disease likewise had, low levels of EFAs.

"The association between fats – meaning saturated, refined w6s (Omega 6), rancid fats, processed oils, and altered fats – and cancer, (but excluding w3s and fresh, natural, unrefined oils) has long been documented. (They) interfere with oxygen use in our cells. Heat, hydrogenation, light, and oxygen produce chemically altered fat products that are toxic to our cells ... These fats kill people. Healing fats in cancer include ... w3s (Omega 3s), enhance oxygen use in cells, decrease tumour formation, slow tumour growth, decrease tumour formation, decrease the spread of cancer cells (metastasis), and extend the patient's survival time. Unsaturated fatty acids in fresh, unheated oils are anti-mutagenic ... W9, w6, w3 are all effective. Saturated fatty acids do not have this protective ability. Heating these oils above 150°C makes them lose their protective power, and they become mutation-causing. ALL mass market oils except virgin olive oil have undergone heating during deodorization ... When we use virgin olive oil or other unrefined oils for sauteing, frying ... we overheat them, destroying their protective, anti-mutagenic properties. ALL hydrogenated and partially hydrogenated products have also been overheated.." – Udo Erasmus (Fats That Heal, Fats That Kill). www.udoerasmus.com

"Our immune system, which is vital for destroying cancer cells, requires EFAs, vitamins C, B6, and A, and zinc to function, and requires an exceptionally rich nutrient supply of ALL essential nutrients for its high level of complex cellular activities. Deficiencies of EFAs and toxic, man-made synthetic drugs that interfere with essential fatty acid functions can create the conditions of fatty degeneration collectively known as cancer." – Erasmus

Dr Rudin believes the Omega 3 story parallels the story of Beriberi & Pellagra. It took them 200 years to accept pellagra was a nutrient deficiency.

"Compared to 100 years ago, Omega 3 is down 80%, B vitamins are estimated to be down to about 50% of the daily requirement. Vitamin B6 consumption may be low as it is removed in grain milling and not replaced. Vitamins B1, B2, B3 and E have also been lost in food processing. Minerals are depleted in a similar way. Fibre is down 75-80%. Antinutrients have increased substantially---saturated fat, 100%; cholesterol, 50%; refined sugar nearly 1000%; salt up to 500%; and funny fat isomers nearly 1,000%." – Dr Rudin.

"Many of my clients with cancer and chronic diseases have restored their health from the application of the simple Budwig diet protocol – cottage cheese and flaxseed oil with freshly ground flax seeds – together with Cessiac and Yuccalive formula, Chinese tonic herbs, meditation, Qigong, emotional stress healing, Emotional Freedom Technique, Qi-healing, sauna (for detoxification), alkaline water, and other Oriental medical therapies.

Dr. Budwig's Diet is the best diet for the prevention and cure of cancer and chronic diseases because it builds the *Ka* pranic body, *Qi life-force* and *Jing*. Flaxseed oil and fish oil are both Yin and Jing tonics that along with Chinese tonic herbs help to strengthen the kidneys, which store and consolidate the Jing. In Chinese medicine, Jing is our essence, it's the quality of our genetic heritage from our parents. As we age, we slowly use up our Jing and we die when our Jing is extinguished. " – Ricardo B Serrano, R.Ac.

Flaxseed Oil: Richest Plant Source of Omega-3 EFA

The light, nutty oil extracted from flaxseeds is the richest known plant source of omega-3 fatty acids – an essential fatty acid that the body needs to live, yet cannot make (in 1992 an analysis of 495 samples of flaxseed grown in three Canadian Prairies provinces: 59% alpha linolenic acid, 15% linoleic acid, 17% oleic acid). To get these vital fatty acids we need to eat foods rich in omega-3. It's easier said than done. Commercial processing of fats and the foods that contain them has almost eliminated this essential fatty acid group from our diets. Dr. Donald Rudin, a renowned researcher into essential fatty acids (*EFA*) and health, estimates that omega-3 fatty acids have been reduced by 80% in our diets in the past 100 years. He theorizes that a deficiency of omega-3 is a leading cause of disease in our twentieth century.

Flaxseed oil, with its plentiful supply of omega-3 fatty acids, may be the preferred way to balance the fatty acids in our favour. It is also ideal for vegetarians who want the benefit of omega-3 without taking fish oils. Referring to the health enhancing effects of omega-3 rich flax oil, Udo Erasmus says: "It is beneficial in treatment programs against all major fatty degenerative conditions, including cancer, cardiovascular disease, diabetes, multiple sclerosis, arthritis, premenstrual syndrome, overweight, and many more."

Who could benefit from omega-3 EFA found in flaxseed oil?

- They may lower levels of total cholesterol: Hundreds of studies show that omega-3 fatty acids can lower triglycerides and cholesterol levels. While most of the studies have been done on fish oil, flaxseed oil is said to have similar results.
- May lower arterial blood pressure: "Over 60 double-blind studies have demonstrated that either fish oil supplements or flaxseed oil are very effective in lowering blood pressure."
- Are converted to prostaglandins, chemicals in the body that regulate a myriad of biochemical functions from inflammatory response to immune function.
- May play an important role in alleviating some skin conditions and digestive disorders.
- Are necessary to the development of the human brain during pregnancy and early childhood. "The omega-3 fat and its derivative, DHA (docosahexaenoic acid), is so essential to a child's development that if a mother and infant are deficient in it, the child's nervous system and immune system may never fully develop...."
- Essential Fatty Acids such as omega-3 from flaxseed oil should be part of a healthy regimen during pregnancy,
- Athletes could benefit from flaxseed oil. "The oil shortens the time necessary for fatigued muscles to recover after exertion, and shortens healing time for bruises, sprains, and other injuries. It increases energy, stamina, and the feeling of vitality, and makes skin soft, hair shiny, and nails strong."
- Flaxseed contains 100 times more lignans than next best source.
- Lignans are phytochemicals found in flaxseed with potential anti-cancer properties.
- Do not cook or fry with flaxseed oil. Use generously in salad dressings, over cooked vegetables or mix with juice.

Quotations from Lothar Hirneise'
Chemotherapy Heals Cancer and the World is Flat

"A tumour is an incredibly ingenious solution on the part of the body."

"Every successful cancer treatment contains three ingredients: thorough detoxification, a change of diet and mental or spiritual work."

"Of course chemotherapy is no fun, but a radical change in your diet and lifestyle is more difficult. That's why so few people survive cancer."

"Cancer cannot exist without stress. One hundred percent impossible!"

"For me the oil-protein diet always serves as the basis of a cancer therapy and please understand that I am not just simply writing this, but that I have carefully chosen my words, as I have become familiar with more than 100 different alternative cancer therapies in recent years, and I have investigated many of them. When Dr. Johanna Budwig died the cancer scene lost one of the last great scientists of the last century, and it behoves each of us to carry her legacy to future generations, so that they as well can profit from the oil-protein diet."

CONCLUDING NOTE by Ricardo B Serrano, R.Ac.: Dr. Budwig Diet that is rich in phosphatides and lipoproteins which are missing in today's standard diet has been used for over 60 years with astonishing curative healing effects to most chronic diseases including cancer. *Food is the best medicine*, according to Oriental medicine. Dr. Budwig diet (The Cancer Solution) integrated with lifestyle dietary change, Chinese tonic herbs, meditation, emotional stress healing, Qi-healing, acupressure, acupuncture, exercise, and Qigong therapy have proven to greatly heal clients with cancer and other chronic health problems for over half a century and will be therapeutically used in the coming years as *safe viable alternative holistic approach.*

I also have personally benefited from the regular use of omega-3 rich flaxseed oil (which I consider as *liquid sunshine*) in restoring my health from symptoms of fatigue, eye pain, skin conditions, allergies, depression and high blood pressure, mainly caused by emotional stress, unhealthy lifestyle and a high fat diet that is high in *trans-fatty acids and low in EFAs*, that I agree wholly with Udo Erasmus' book *Fats that Heal Fats that Kill* when he says, "Healing fats are *required*, together with other nutrients, to prevent and reverse so-called "incurable" degenerative disease: heart disease, cancer, and type 2 diabetes. Healing fats help reverse arthritis, obesity, PMS, allergies, asthma, skin conditions, fatigue, yeast and fungal infections, addictions, certain types of mental illness, and many other conditions. Good fats also enhance athletic performances, skin beauty, longevity and energy levels. Contrary to popular belief based on advertising hype, the most dangerous fats are typically found in margarine, shortenings, and heated oils."

With these powerful knowledge at your disposal now, disregard your unnecessary fear because *you have the keys to healing*.

The cause and cure of cancer is within you!

Book References:
Cancer: The Problem and the Solution by Dr. Johanna Budwig and Lothar Hirneise, 2008.

The Cancer Solution by Dr. Robert E. Willner, MD, PhD., 1993.

Fats that Heal Fats that Kill by Udo Erasmus, 1993.

The Sahhu or Immortal Golden Lightbody and Its Soul Powers

The Sahhu (also called "immortal golden lightbody") I'm referring to is the ultimate goal of Taoist, Buddhist, Mayan, Shaivite, Egyptian internal alchemy practices, Qigong, Merkaba meditation, and the Hathor's Holographic Sound Healing which will be your actualized crystalized replica after the so called "death" of the physical body. The following statements will try to answer *"How do I manifest an immortal body and its soul powers?"* which is both relevant to any aspiring practitioner of yoga and energy healing, and layman because the successful outcome of energy healing depends upon the *"energy body"* of the healer and *"energy body"* of the client. Whole body enlightenment is also dependent on the development of your immortal energy body. I hope that my little contribution in this article will assist you as its mentioned technologies have absolutely assisted me in my fruitful real life journey to the Tao, Natural Way, by realizing and actualizing my immortal Self.

Tao, Qi and Your Energy Body

Tao is a way of life, based on the natural spiritual science of Qi flow. Cultivating Qi flow spontaneously unfolds one's original spiritual essence. It empowers us to shape our worldly destiny. *Is your energy body ready to flow to the incoming solar 5th element Sun fully manifesting in 2012? Did you even know that you have an energy body?*

Your energy body occupies the same space as your solid physical body, but with a distinctly different structure. Your energy or Qi body has an invisible network of vital organ meridians and deeper core channels. Your Qi flows through these channels and your innate intelligence (your inner voice) shapes this Qi into a physical body, into your feelings, your sexual impulses, your thoughts, your highest intuitions, your everything. Qi is the intelligence that controls your genetic code unfoldment. Maybe that is why so many thousands of people get miraculous healings from Qigong, even after doctors have written them off as dead or sentenced them to life with an incurable illness! Eventually, this Qi technology will become standard information in the medicine, psychology, and religion of the new millennium. *Why wait for the medical establishment to catch up with snail paced speed?*

An important addition to Qigong, Qi-healing and meditation in the building of the *Sahhu* or *immortal golden lightbody* which will speed up its development is through the practice of the Hathor's emotional mastery technique, Merkaba meditation, Holographic Sound Healing, and *Sun gazing* elaborated in the following article *Sun Yoga and Its Healing and Enlightenment Aspects.*

Whole Body Enlightenment and Energy Healing Process

Since the 1980s, I have started pursuing the truth through the original Taoist Traditional Chinese medical philosophy, as an acupuncturist, in regards to the concept of Qi, the bio-electromagnetic energy which underlies matter for healing and spiritual development. In my quest for the underlying process of natural healing together with spiritual enlightenment, I have studied with enlightened Masters – Master Choa Kok Sui, Master Li Jun Feng (Sheng Zhen Qigong), Master Miguel Nator, Master Mantak Chia, Master Michael Winn, Master Ou Wen Wei, Baba Muktananda, Swami Lakshmanjoo, Lama Tantrapa, Holographic Sound Healer Paul Hubbert, Sun Yogi Hira Ratan Manek, and Alton Kamadon of the Melchizedek Method – whom I am forever grateful and acknowledged for their definite contribution to my whole body enlightenment. During the course of my studies with each of their technologies, I have used my body as the laboratory to integrate and test their theories and hands on application before I taught and applied their human energy sciences of the 21st century to my acupuncture clients in my practice.

The whole body enlightenment process which happens at the same time during the creation of your *"golden light body"* is mapped out for us by the ancient Taoist masters through the present day Taoist Master, Mantak Chia of the Universal Tao, and one of his senior instructors, Michael Winn of the Healing Tao. The Taoist Yoga masters Mantak Chia and Michael Winn have taught me the following powerful Taoist internal alchemy technologies: Microcosmic Orbit, inner smile, healing sounds, sexual alchemy, opening of the eight extraordinary channels (governor, functional, thrusting, yin bridge and regulator, yang bridge and regulator, and belt channels), iron shirt, fusion of the five elements, and cosmic qigong. Their greatest contribution to my spiritual growth is laying the foundation for the actualization of my immortal body which can withstand the high voltage of love and energy from the God Source making it safe for my grounded physical body to practice advanced meditation techniques.

According to Michael Winn, *"The Daoist concept of immortality does not mean you live physically forever. Immortality means you achieve spiritual integration of your authentic self (zhenren).*

Your authentic Self is immortal because it has the power to survive the transition of physical death and continues its life in higher dimensions. This process requires integrating the physical body's sexual essence (jing), the energy body (qi), and the spirit body (shen) into a functional state of total openness (wu) to the multi-dimensionality of the present moment. The spiritual power of manifestation hidden within the sexual essence is most critical to cultivating what is known as a "golden light body" or the authentic immortal Self. Without the sexual essence being properly cultivated, the crystallization of one's spirit does not occur.

Cultivating this high level of harmony and balance requires a progressive training of the body's sexual essence (jing), the mind (qi), and the spirit (shen) within a state of total openness (wu). The purpose of the training is to accelerate transformations that might take Nature many lifetimes to accomplish. Inner Alchemy is a precise step-by-step process, and each step builds on the next. Using One Cloud's structure, I have added my own refinements based on study with many masters and decades of practice and teaching.

I found the Daoist Water and Fire alchemy practices to be more body-centered, and thus more grounded and appropriate for Westerners at this time. They emphasize the "below" realizing the "above" is hidden within itself. One Cloud's Daoist Water and Fire approach translates into the liberation of the spirit hidden within matter-body, and the rebirthing of deep earth consciousness. It is the feminine discovering that yang fire is its true inner nature. I am sharing them because I feel they penetrate and resolve the problem of the BODY which plagues so many meditators seeking perfect union with Spirit.

I myself once had this problem, of wanting to get out of my body so that my meditations would be more perfect. It was a rude awakening for me to realize my desire was not for transcendence, it was at core escapist. What was I escaping? The difficulty of staying here, of living in a body. I was escaping my failure to recognize and accept the spiritual nature of the physical body. I falsely believed if I opened my third eye and went out my crown, that my spiritual journey was complete. My kundalini was wide open, but I was only using it to go one way, instead of seeing its circular-cyclical nature.

I was denying how essential the body is to full enlightenment. I now make a distinction between those achieving "head enlightenment" and those achieving "whole body enlightenment". They are very different experiences. All meditation methods are wonderful gifts. Alchemy is a special kind of meditative gift that is dynamic, accepts the sexual nature of the body, and seeks to refine the entire body into an elevated spiritual state."

The Arhat Masters Choa Kok Sui and Miguel Nator from my native country, the Philippines, have taught me the following: Advanced Pranic Healing, Pranic Psychotherapy, Arhatic yoga, Meditation on Twin Hearts, Triangles Work, Pranic crystal healing, and Winged Unicorn meditation for clairvoyance. Their greatest contribution is the use of color and prana for cosmic healing or Qigong together with spiritual enlightenment through Arhatic Yoga and Yoga of Immortality which also laid the foundation for the development of the *"golden immortal light body"*.

According to Master Choa Kok Sui, *"Very advanced pranic healers may have an inner aura of more than fifty meters and the energy body is extremely refined.*

If the healer has a very refined energy body, then more pranic energy can be projected to the patient without causing pranic congestion. For example, a very advanced pranic healer can increase the inner aura of the patient from 3 inches to about 3 feet without causing discomfort or pranic congestion on the patient. A very advanced pranic healer can project a tremendous amount of refined pranic energy which are assimilable within a very short period of time, resulting in rapid healing of patients.

Students of pranic healing can become more powerful, effective healers by regularly practicing Arhatic Meditation. Arhatic Meditation causes chakras to become bigger and to move a lot faster. It causes the energy body and the auras of the practitioner to become bigger, denser, and more refined. Thereby, it enables the practitioner to heal very fast and more effectively.

There are several spiritual or yogic systems of activating the chakras and awakening the kundalini. Arhatic Meditation is one of the systems that systematically, safely and rapidly activates the chakras and awakens the kundalini."

IMPORTANT NOTE: I believe that the one important necessary technology for *"whole body enlightenment"* that is missing in the Merkaba meditation is the lack of laying the foundation for the development of the *"energy body"* or *"Qi body"* based on the Lower Dan Tien (the mother of the 8 Extraordinary Vessels) – the *"electromagnetic body"* according to Merkaba meditation – which the Taoist and Arhatic Yoga laid the foundation for the development of the *"golden immortal light body"* with internal alchemy practices such as sexual alchemy, inner alchemy inner smile/healing sounds and microcosmic orbit meditation – also known as *"opening the golden flower"* and *"embryo or womb breathing"* – with fusion of the five elements Qigong. I strongly and personally believe that the Merkaba meditation, holographic sound healing, Sun gazing, and Qigong are the higher levels of Meditation and Qigong Mastery – integrated as gifts from the Hathors, Master Thoth, Master Mei Ling, Pan Gu, and the lineage of the Eight Taoist Immortals – considering the fact that many Buddhists, Christians, and Sufis study Tao because it helps ground spirit into the body. *What made me say these bold innovative statements?* I have decided to fulfill the integration of these powerful technologies because it is my chosen mission with the Masters of Light, and the integrated program works in practice. So be it!

Alton Kamadon has taught me the Melchizedek Method which uses the Hologram of Love merkabah, the Zenith light body, path of vision for multi-dimensional healing and ascension. His greatest contribution is the use of the Orionis Zenith Lightbody Merkabah, path of vision, the metatronic waveform pattern and yantras with the 33 chakra system for ascension and healing.

According to my late beloved Ascended Master Alton Kamadon, *"These sacred symbols and patterns, embedded into very powerful super powerball love spheres, will have the effect of quickening our receptive brain cells to receive the highest levels of thought forms available to us through our superconsciousness Metatronic waveform pineal gland, and electromagnetic antennae connected to Orionis. We already activate the most powerful merkabah on Earth. Now we must expand heart and consciousness to accommodate the incoming 5th dimension love and divine thoughts, to manifest our "Zenith Light Body".*

The technique used to encode ourselves with these new sacred super powerballs is called "One Path of Vision". Through this technique we will merge the inner eye with our 3D eyes, and at the same time connect the heart to the soul.

"One Path of Vision" will not only allow us to accelerate our personal ascension, but collectively we will release these powerful 5th dimensional encoded sacred super powerballs of love into the planetary 555 human Cosmic Christ Consciousness electromagnetic thought grid to serve the continuous advancement of humanity.

The Mayan elders have talked recently about the incoming solar 5th element Sun fully manifesting in 2012. They are adamant that it will manifest and our new world will be of love and light.

The continuous Level 5 Melchizedek Method presentations will open human consciousness to evolve and accelerate towards this divine moment in our history.

Level 5 will be a very visual presentation of 3D animations on screen, allowing these new sacred powerballs to be drawn in through the eyes. Our eyes will then connect through God's Eye and into the Creator Lord's Elohim Eye. We will manifest our "Zenith Light Body" of superconsciousness through the love of our soul.

Level 5 is by far the most expansive quantum leap in this spiritual work to date. Because of the visual nature of Level 5 we will be drawn much more deeply into the complexities of the Orionis 5th dimensional consciousness and unconditional love."

Finally, over the span of thirty years of meditation, cosmic medical Qigong and hands-on application in my acupuncture practice, I believe that I have manifested my *Sahhu* or *immortal golden lightbody* and its soul powers especially for *whole body enlightenment, healing and ascension* through the application and integration of the Taoist Wuji Qigong, Pan Gu Shen Gong, Maitreya (Shiva) Shen Gong, Sheng Zhen Qigong, Siddha meditation, Qi Dao, pranic healing, Merkaba meditation, Emotional Freedom Technique, Sun gazing, and the Hathor's emotional mastery technique and Holographic Sound Healing. This integration resulted in my Vancouver Qigong Mastery meditation and quantum multi-dimensional healing protocol which I developed and founded for the benefit of those students who wanted a spirit-body-mind technology that is integrated, well rounded, attainable, rewarding and has safe outcome.

Is it possible to attain an immortal body? A definite yes. However, you are the only one who can complete your whole body enlightenment and nobody else. All I or any healer/teacher can do is guide you, nevertheless, this most worthwhile work takes time and is its own reward because on a personal level it is the only thing you can take with you. You can't take your money or your reputation or your kids or your house or anything. You can only take your essence. And if you have not integrated it you can't even take the fragments of your essence with you at death. Until you integrate your essence into an *immortal golden light body*, you don't even own yourself, you're just a temporary composite of various spirits. Ultimately, I believe that once you have actualized your *"energy body"* and attained *whole body enlightenment*, your reincarnation cycle comes to an end.

Lastly, the Hathors and ascended masters, and the powers of your Higher Self, the "soul body of your immortal golden lightbody," in addition to ascension, whole body enlightenment and cosmic healing, can give you advice, protection, and guidance in your life. If you can, constantly feel the soul's presence. Truth can only be known by EXPERIENCE, not by belief or thoughts.

Golden Immortal Lightbody

Sun Yoga and Its Healing and Enlightenment Aspects

"The most 'biologically active' part of sunlight is the ultraviolet.
It is absolutely critical for optimal health" - Zane R. Kime, M.D.

Most people in the West are not familiar of Sun Yoga as a disciplined practice of safe Sun gazing, safe sunbathing, and drinking sun charged water and are not aware of its healing aspects.

To maximize the energetic healing effect of the sun for chronic physical, mental and emotional ailments caused by sunlight and primordial Qi energy deficiency, I have combined the disciplined practice of Sun gazing (**ten seconds Sun gazing**), sunbathing and Qigong at sunrise daily for healing, whole body enlightenment, and transformation of consciousness.

The Sunlight and Eye model below with excerpts on the eyes, sunlight and well-being, and ultraviolet light from the sun derived from Dr. Jacob Liberman's book I believe explain scientifically the healing aspects and the process behind the safe Sun gazing and safe sunbathing practice as promoted by my Sun gazing and sunbathing teacher Sun Yogi Hira Ratan Manek.

Some personal benefits of attending the workshop in Marinduque, Philippines – the *heart-shaped island of the Philippines* – are magnified awareness, sense of inner guidance, deepened harmony with the flow of life and the peace of one's own true rhythms, heightened sense of telepathy, increased experience of synchronicity and alignment, participation with a global family of awakening, entrainment of one's bio-magnetic field and electro-chemical circuitry with that of the Earth's and Beyond, conscious connection of our hearts with Nature's hand of balance.

As a natural born Filipino, I personally have lived in Buenavista, Marinduque, Philippines and frequently visit this *"inner heart"* of the Philippines Islands to synchronize myself with its powerful vortex of *Love* and *"Qi"* energy frequency – one of the twelve energy grid areas for space-time transcription, and areas of protocommunication according to *Keys of Enoch* **Key 215:70** – and attune with nature, my *'Higher Self'*, Masters of Light and the *"golden mean" Cosmic Heart Spiral of Love* for *ascension, whole body enlightenment and cosmic healing*, and most of all to detoxify and rejuvenate through Qigong and Sun gazing.

Sunlight and Eye Model with Hypothalamus at the center of all bodily functions

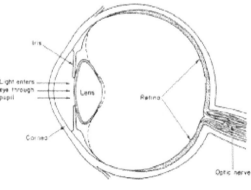

- Hypothalamus
- Autonomic Nervous System
- Parasympathetic Nervous System
- Pineal Gland
- Pituitary Gland
- Endocrine System

The Eyes, Sunlight and our Well-Being

These findings, along with those of many other highly respected scientists and physicians, seem to indicate that the human body is truly a living photocell that is energized by the sun's light, the nutrient of humankind. Since light is recognized as having a profound effect on all living things, and since our perception of light is by way of our eyes, it becomes evident that the function of the eyes may not be for "*seeing*" alone.

Light enters the eyes not only to serve vision, but to go directly to the body's biological clock within the hypothalamus. The hypothalamus controls the nervous system and endocrine system, whose combined effects regulate all biological functions in humans. In addition, the hypothalamus controls most of the body's regulatory functions by monitoring light-related information and sending it to the pineal, which then uses this information to cue other organs about light conditions in the environment. In other words, the hypothalamus acts as a puppet master who, quietly and out of sight, controls most of the functions that keep the body in balance.

All the body's systems relate to each other in a constant state of flux, with the hypothalamus at the center. The hypothalamus interfaces between mind and body, coordinating the readiness of both, affecting our consciousness, and thereby controlling our constant state of preparedness. This critical maintenance of body harmony is affected by synchronizing the body's vital functions with the environmental conditions, or, as some people say, "*becoming one with the universe*."

Why we need UV light from the sun:

UV light activates vitamin D synthesis.
UV light lowers blood pressure.
UV light increases heart "performance".
UV light improves ECG and blood parameters in persons suffering from arteriosclerosis.
UV light lowers cholesterol counts.
UV light helps in weight loss.
UV light is effective against psoriasis.
UV light is effective with numerous other ailments (Krudsen in his book Light Therapy lists 165 diseases).
UV light promotes the production of sex hormones.
UV light activates an important skin hormone (Solitrole).
UV light is a nutrient just as vitamins and minerals.

Has Science Made a Mistake?

What does nature say about all this? The research papers don't seem to address the fact that humans evolved under natural sunlight. Are we supposed to dismiss five million years of evolution because science doesn't understand the supreme wisdom of nature? In modern times, all of a sudden, ultraviolet light is "dangerous" and should be avoided at all costs. We live in houses with no ultraviolet light. When we leave our houses, we put on our glasses, contacts, or sunglasses, which block most of the UV light. We drive in cars that also block UV light. We work all day in offices and receive no UV there either. Then at night we turn on our grossly distorted man-made lights - still no UV light.

When we finally take a break and get out in the sun, what do we do? We put on our sunglasses and cover our skin with sunscreens - just to make sure we aren't exposed to these hazardous rays. A lot of people are now petrified to go out in the natural sunshine without some form of protection. Is there a possibility that maybe - just maybe - we have gone a little too far? Is it possible that science may have made a mistake?

"The most 'biologically active' part of sunlight is the ultraviolet. It is absolutely critical for optimal health"
- Zane R. Kime, M.D., Swannanoa Health Report, issues 2 & 3.

(excerpts from Light, Medicine of the Future by Dr. Jacob Liberman)

"The sun is central to our well being and health. The light and heat from the sun are indispensable to all nature. Humanity is also part of nature and needs sunlight for health and well being, for vitality and happiness. There is a considerable body of scientific evidence demonstrating that "sunlight may play a key role in preventing and ameliorating a number of serious degenerative and infection diseases, including cancers of the breast, colon, ovaries and prostate; diabetes; high blood pressure; heart disease; multiple sclerosis; osteoporosis; psoriasis; rickets and tuberculosis."

A closer study of the action of solar radiation on the body might well reveal the nature of cancer immunity." - Dr. Richard Hobday, Healing Sun

Sun Yoga is basically a simple safe healing and spiritual enlightenment practice to learn, anyone can do it!

As a Sun Yoga Facilitator, pranic healer and Qigong practitioner, I believe that the HRM phenomenon becomes possible when the primordial Qi energy supplied by the sun via the eyes and chakras is restored in the body to normal levels. Eyes are used as windows to the soul. The following articles are different popular hypotheses which offer an explanation for the HRM phenomenon:

According to Hira Ratan Manek, the body cells are photo-voltaic, just as solar panel cells are. Once you start grooming the cells to harness the power of the sun, you can generate the energy needed for your body from sunlight. As it is, whatever you eat are secondary sources of energy, all of them drawing their reserves from sunlight, reminds Manek.

Tapping the sun has a more long-run benefit, he says. To explain it further, he draws your attention to the human brain, which he calls a brainuter (from brain plus computer). People hardly use the full capability of their brain cells; the usage can be determined scientifically through MRI scans, he adds.

The talent that is inherent in every human being is the software of the brainuter, and the mind is its keyboard and mouse. Finally, it needs power, which comes from the sun.

This power effectively reaches the brain through the eyes, says Manek, and thus, all he requests anyone who is interested in his 'Sun gazing' theory through what is now globally known as the HRM (Hira Ratan Manek) Phenomenon, is to gaze at the sun every day.

Sun gazing generates Vitamin A in the body, says Manek, which would lead to enhanced sight, and prevention of many eye diseases, and cure too. He says in three months time, the body gains sound mental health, which is characterised by no fear, more self-confidence and a balanced mind. It also derides the body of evil traits like greed, anger and jealousy. All this, he asserts, have been scientifically established. Manek adds that mental wellness is the key to global peace.

Continue the practice for six months, and the sun could start healing diseases, claims Manek. He says that harnessing the energy of the sun is the essence of Reiki, Pranic Healing and even, Feng Shui. "*In this, however, you don't need a third party. You do the healing yourself.*"

He lists a number of disease conditions including cancer, AIDS, diabetes, obesity, osteoporosis and a string of mental and ageing disorders that can be addressed by solar healing.

The sun is both spiritual light and material form, the purest manifestation of the oneness of that which is visible with the invisible, of matter and energy. The sun is deified cosmic energy, so are crystals, and potentially, so are we. The true worship of the sun is based upon attunement not only to the light, but to the ultimate essence of all existence: the force behind the force, the impersonal energy of the cosmos. The sun is the light body of the earth, just as our light bodies exist in the Soul Star region above the tops of our heads. There are billions of suns, just as there are billions of people. The fact remains that the animating force behind it all, is Divine Presence. That essence can be attuned to and integrated into our twelve chakra system by practicing the ancient common worship of the sun.

The sun is a gateway of light, an opening in the universe to other dimensions, to greater galactic spheres. The Sun Meditations are one way of integrating the Divine Essence into our beings. When human consciousness relates to the soul of the sun, to the light body of our earth, to the Great Central Sun nurturing our tiny star, and to the cosmic force beyond it all, the Crystalline Essence is experienced and shines through.

Reference: The Crystal Transmission, A Synthesis of Light by Katrina Raphaell, 1990

Taoist Astral Healing hypothesis:

From Master Mantak Chia's Taoist Astral Healing's alchemical Qigong point of view, the sun and moon energies were a major influence in the development of human consciousness as it evolved from more primitive life forms (mammals and reptiles).

The development of the neocortex as well as the etheric brain is the product of 500 million years of evolution. About 100 million years ago, the multiple-layer structure of the neocortex was formed. This process is still evolving. At the highest level of awareness, the neocortex expands energetically beyond the physical boundaries of the skull. This expanded "aural brain" connects one to the higher, godly levels, and facilitates clairvoyance vision and enlightenment. These auras have been depicted as golden crowns or halos in paintings of Christian saints.

The sun has a connection with the third eye and pituitary gland. It is the star connected with consciousness and future vision. It functions as a source of consciousness and compassion and as a gate to the higher universe. The sun is also connected to the heart center, and has a controlling and regulating effect on the heart energy.

The sun is a gateway to a higher dimension and to higher energy frequencies in the universe. The earth and moon are used to keep the grounding and to integrate high frequency energies in the physical body. In order to pass through the sun gateway, balance and integration of the underlying energies are required.

The spiral shown by the movement of the sun, and planets as they move through the galaxy shows a similarity to the structure of DNA. DNA is the fundamental building block of all living cells. Many Taoist astrologers believe that DNA also contains a complicated transmitter and receiver system that picks up the continuous energetic changes in the solar system and Milky Way.

Taoists believe that the food sources with the purest form of energy are the green leafy vegetables, which have taken sunlight directly into their cells. Rather than waiting until the solar energy is processed through plants, the Taoist goes directly to the source of this primordial energy. The Immortal Taoist Masters cherish the yoga Sun gazing activity, along with Qigong, as the keys to health, energy and longevity.

Why the health care system is broken

Almost all drugs are toxic and are designed only to treat symptoms and not to cure anyone. - Dr. Alan Greenberg, MD

Over-prescribed and adverse side effects

Doctors are rewarded for prescribing drugs. Big pharmaceutical companies are known to hand out "consulting agreements" worth more than your annual salary to doctors who prescribe their drugs like candy. This is one of the worst practices I can think of that drives a stake right through the heart of healthcare's credibility.

And unfortunately it seems people accept it and take pills for everything.

Have a headache? Take a pill. A rash? Take a pill. Sore muscle? Take a pill. Tired? Take a pill. Overwhelmed? Take a pill. The list goes on and on.

Why do people these days feel the need to take a pill for every ache and pain they have?
What do they think people did before these medications were around?
Why are doctors so easy to prescribe a pill for everything?
Is it an easy way out?
Are they getting paid from the drug companies to prescribe them?

"Why don't doctors talk about preventing disease." - Dr Carolyn Dean

Overprescribing of drugs by medical doctors is what makes a health care system broken. No wonder there is an opioid epidemic, Alzheimer's and mental health crisis caused by overprescription of painkillers and antidepressants by medical doctors.

"You need to understand that they want you sick and dying, expensively." - Dr Carolyn Dean, MD, ND

There are natural medicine alternatives to prescription drugs for your general health problems without side-effects such as acupuncture, herbs, acupressure, Qigong, diet, exercise and intranasal light therapy.

The healing process is completely natural in harnessing the power of the body to repair itself. Natural medicine does no harm, respects the natural power of the body to heal, addresses the causes of illness rather than the symptoms (at the mitochondrial level), encourages self-responsibility for health, considers the fundamental health factors, and definitely promotes prevention of diseases. - Ricardo B Serrano, R.Ac.

70-80% of people are magnesium deficient. Magnesium deficiency is a public health crisis of epic proportions. Mitochondria are the powerhouses of cells, producing energy in the Krebs cycle. - Dr. Carolyn Dean, MD, ND

Coenzyme Q10 and *Magnesium* are essential nutrients required by mitochondria to generate ATP (adenosine triphosphate), and best integrated with intranasal light therapy for healing chronic diseases such as depression, fatigue, diabetes, hypertension, migraine, PMS, insomnia, arthritis, stroke, osteoporosis, asthma, dementia and cancer.

Mitochondrial dysfunction is the root cause of chronic diseases.

For more information on intranasal light therapy, read *Return to Oneness with the Tao*, and *The Cure and Cause of Cancer*.

Conclusion:

Therefore, from the above hypotheses and the Taoist alchemical point of view regarding the effect of the sun to the evolution of our consciousness, the connection of the sun with the third eye and pituitary gland, the sun as a gateway to the higher energy frequencies in the universe, the effect of the sun to human's DNA, and as a primordial source of energy, are I believe the valid explanations of the HRM phenomenon for our healing, spiritual enlightenment and evolution of our consciousness. Another way to stimulate the *mitochondria* (powerhouse of cells) to produce *adenosine triphosphate* (ATP) - Qi energy - is by *intranasal light therapy with* Coenzyme Q10 and magnesium supplementation.

"By the year 2001 will be in more of the year than out. By 2012 earth's entire orbit will be in the photon belt. The most intense part of the transition will be when our Sun moves fully into the Photon Belt in late 1998 or early 1999 – the apex of the predicted earth changes. The action of the photon belt, will also have significant effect on the pineal gland. That's why everyone's psychic energy is starting to ramp up. Barbara HC theorizes that the photon action will have a lot to do with unlocking and decoding our DNA for the next leap in evolution. Understanding these cycles is crucial to the awakening process we are all experiencing
and will help reduce the physical, mental and emotional shock of this transition." – Barbara Hand Clow, Age of Light

"Through Solar Initiation they will be able to see the luminosity of the Great Spirit ... through Solar Initiation, the sleeping body of humankind can be awakened ... "Hunab K'u (Creator) will flash like lightening that will pierce through the shadows that envelop the human race. Let us prepare to receive the light of
knowledge" (paraphrased Mayan prophesy)."

"We create our Reality. For whatever reason or purpose, the mass consciousness of humanity is embracing linear time and creating a very limited reality. As each of us shifts out of the mass consciousness, it helps to change the whole. Love and Honor your Mother Earth. Receive the Galactic Synchronization Beam from the Sun. Sing the song of your Soul. Listen to your Heart."

"The body cells are photo-voltaic, just as solar panel cells are. Once you start grooming the cells to harness the power of the sun, you can generate the energy needed for your body from sunlight."

"Eyes are the Sun Energy's entry door to the human brain.
They are also known as the windows of the soul." – Hira Ratan Manek

GAYATRI MANTRA
*Om Bhur Bhuvah Svah Tat Savitur Varenyam
Bhargo Devasya Dhimahi Dhiyo Yo Nah Pracodayat*

"**Let us meditate on the light of the Sun which represents God,
and may our thoughts be inspired by that Divine Light**."

IMPORTANT NOTE: The Sun Gazing Practice is an important necessary solar initiation technique to receive the Galactic Synchronization Beam from the *Ka* (essence) of our Father Sun which connect us and Mother Earth to the galactic core, Hunab Ku, the One Giver of Movement and Measure, developing our *Sahhu* or *immortal golden lightbody in the process.*

10 seconds *Sun Gazing has to be done safely, thus, the need for facilitation by a Sun Yoga Facilitator. Grounding to Mother Earth through Qigong and barefoot walking before Sun gazing is necessary to avoid Qi deviation. Sun gazing after 1 hour after sunrise or before 1 hour before sunset is a **no-no**!*

The information in this book is for educational and reference purposes only. Its contents are not intended as, nor are they a substitute for, personal one-on-one diagnosis or treatment by, or consultation with, a licensed health care practitioner or Qigong expert.

NOTABLE SAYINGS

Like oil in sesame seeds,
butter in cream,
water in the river bed,
fire in tinder,
the Self dwells within.
Realize the Self through meditation.
Shvetashvatara Upanishad

God Consciousness is not achieved by means of the scriptures,
nor is it achieved by the Grace of your Master.
God Consciousness is only achieved by your own subtle awareness."
– Yoga Vashistha

He is the real Guru
Who can reveal the form of the formless
before your eyes;
Who teaches the simple path,
without rites or ceremonies;
Who does not make you close
your doors, and hold your breath,
and renounce the world;
Who makes you perceive
the Supreme Spirit
wherever the mind attaches itself;
Who teaches you to be still
in the midst of all your activities.
Fearless, always immersed in bliss,
he keeps the spirit of yoga
in the midst of enjoyments.
KABIR

"The Five Agreements are tools to change your world. If you are *impeccable with your word*, if you *don't take anything personally*, if you *don't make assumptions*, if you *always do your best*, and if you are *skeptical while listening*, there won't be any more war in your head; there will be peace." – don Miguel Ruiz

"Truly, flax oil lubricates our way into eternal life." – hero of Ehm Welk's novel
"Wherever flax seed becomes a regular food item among the people,
there will be better health." – Mahatma Gandhi

Feeling is the fuel for transmutation and the food for evolution and growth.

*The central pivotal point is achieving the vibratory field of high coherency,
unconditional love and unconditional acceptance.* – Hathors

Let Love Light Your Path, Truth Guide Your Way and Joy Sing From Your Soul. – *Sananda*

"Pan Gu Shengong, also known as the Heaven, Earth, Sun and Moon Qigong, has its fundamental philosophy and practice rooted in kindness and charity. It is designed to absorb the essence of Qi (energy) from the universe. It regulates and intensifies life force and the human immune system.

PGSG, which is a complete set of Qigong exercises, consists of a Moving Form, a Non-moving Form (meditation) and an Advanced condensed Form. The Moving Form is the basis, which only takes you 20 minutes to finish. The Non-moving Form is a meditation, focusing on the regulation of the nervous system and the spirit. The Advanced condensed Form is a condensed form which takes less time but produces more powerful effect.

Qi-healing is an energy treatment offered by a Qigong Master. The energy emitted by the Master works on the patients' body, fighting the disease and improving the immune system." – Pan Gu Shengong Master Ou Wen Wei

"*Primordial Qi Gong opens the heart to the true force of unconditional love emanating from Wuji, the Supreme Unknown.*" – Wuji Qigong Master Michael Winn

"In the Sheng Zhen forms of qigong, opening one's heart is the primary purpose. The qi is the vehicle of unconditional love, of Sheng Zhen.

"Love can transform people's hearts. Love can dissolve hate. Love can affect the environment. Unconditional love is the best medicine and the highest power." – Sheng Zhen Qigong Master Li Jun Feng

"*Historically, all styles originated at one time or another from a primordial foundation of Qigong that was deeply rooted in Shamanic Medicine Dances.*" – Qi Dao Master Lama Tantrapa

"The hologram of love (or *Merkaba*) is the sacred geometric pattern which gave birth to the whole universe. It is based on unconditional love, so it must be the pattern of unconditional love, because everything in the universe resonates to it, no matter what it is or what dimension it's in. That means that you and I, as human beings, also have that pattern within us, so we are actually walking, talking unconditional love. We always have been, we've just never recognized it.

With the breath and thought intention, the hologram of love will obey your every command and you will transverse the angles of linear time and into the higher dimensions of no time and endless love." – Merkaba Master Alton Kamadon

"Spiritual energy is needed for expansion of consciousness and traveling in the inner worlds. Stillness and awareness are not enough. No spiritual energy, no expansion of consciousness. Spiritual empowerment or Shaktipat is the transference of tremendous spiritual energy to enable the consciousness of the disciple to be able to travel to the different levels of the inner world. This transference of tremendous spiritual energy is called spiritual initiation in modern esoteric books. Shaktipat is an Indian term for spiritual empowerment." – Master Choa Kok Sui

"One must seek the shortest way and the fastest means to get back home – to turn the spark within into a blaze, to be merged in and to identify with that greater fire which ignited the spark." – Bhagawan Nityananda

"*Qi-healing and Enlightenment Qigong forms are both meditation in motion practices to achieve spiritual oneness.*" – Ricardo B. Serrano, R.Ac.

Enlightenment Qigong Forms for Returning to Oneness

Acharya Ricardo welcomes you to this non-denominational website that is dedicated to the spread of non-denominational integrative Enlightenment Qigong forms throughout the world for awakening our true inner selves to return to oneness by opening the heart to unconditional love.

The Enlightenment Qigong (Wuji Qigong) forms synthesized and taught by Master Ricardo B. Serrano, R.Ac., a Qi-healer and certified Qigong instructor, are Pan Gu Shen Gong, Primordial Wuji Qigong, Sheng Zhen Wuji Yuan Gong, and Maitreya (Shiva) Shen Gong supplemented with spontaneous Tibetan Shamanic Qigong, a formless Qigong, together with Shaktipat meditation.

May the regular practice of these four complementary Enlightenment Qigong forms together with the formless spontaneous Tibetan Shamanic Qigong and Shaktipat meditation provide spiritual healing and enlightenment to yourself as they have provided to myself and fellow practitioners spiritual enlightenment and healing by purifying the physical body, calming the emotions, and opening the heart/ elevating the spirit, together with building the Three Treasures – Jing , Qi and Shen.

Through their ancient lineages, these four Enlightenment Qigong forms, applied individually or in combination, have been clinically tested and proven together with the formless spontaneous Tibetan Shamanic Qigong and Shaktipat meditation by myself and their practitioners to provide a strong basic foundation for understanding and experiencing spiritual enlightenment and healing self and others through contemplations with movements, and non-moving meditation to return to oneness by connecting oneself with heaven, earth and humanity.

Enlightenment is another term for Qigong state, ascension, illumination or spiritual oneness, wherein the incarnated soul is achieving a higher degree of oneness with the higher soul, and a certain degree of oneness with God and oneness with all, experienced as expansion of consciousness accompanied with blissful joy, inner peace and quiet mind.

The Supreme Being is known by many names God, Origin, Primal Mother, Tao, Shiva, Pan Gu, Dream Being, Source at the center of all sacred space called Wu Ji, Void, Nothingness, supreme unknown, the primordial space.

Qigong is an interexchange of Qi (universal life force) between men and the universe. As an integral system of Oriental medicine, Qigong is based on the coherence of human energy fields within the universal flow of Qi, or life force. Qi comes from the power of love, Qi and love are never separate, and Love is the Source of All. Enlightenment Qigong is also called Wuji Qigong, meaning "skill at entering the Supreme Unknown."

To have a greater sense of well-being and spiritual awakening, it is necessary to include and practice Shaktipat meditation with spontaneous formless Tibetan Shamanic Qigong, the root of the entire Qigong tree, with the six branches of the Qigong tree and the most proven enlightenment Qigong forms – Taoist, Buddhist, Medical, Martial Arts, Confucianist and Tantric Qigong – shown from the Pan Gu Shengong, Primordial Wuji Qigong, Sheng Zhen Wuji Yuan Gong, Maitreya (Shiva) Shen Gong, and Qi Dao martial arts forms practiced since time immemorial.

It is in blessing that you are blessed. It is in giving that you receive. It is in going with the flow of Qi and surrendering to it that you master being in the flow. This is the law or principle - "*Where energy flows, awareness follows*" - followed by Qigong masters, and the way to become enlightened!

BOOK REFERENCES

Molecules of Emotion, Why You Feel the Way You Feel," by Dr. Candace Pert, 1997.

You Hold the Keys to Your Healing by Dr. Nelie Johnson, 2011.

The Hathor Material by Tom Kenyon & Virginia Essene, 1996.

The Ancient Secret of The Flower of Life Volume 2 by Drunvalo Melchizedek, 2000.

Vibrational Medicine: New Choices for Healing Ourselves by Dr. Richard Gerber, 1988.

The Healing Tones of Crystal Bowls by Renee Brodie, 1996.

Bringers of the Dawn – Teachings from the Pleidians by Barbara Marciniak

Crystalline Transmission by Katrina Raphaell, 1989.

Flower Essences and Vibrational Healing by Kevin Ryerson, 1983.

Your Body Doesn't Lie by Dr. John Diamond, 1989.

Healing Sounds by Jonathan Goldman, 2002.

The Soul Garden by Deborah Van Dyke.

Music and Sound in the Healing Arts by John Beauliu, 1995.

Steven Halpern with Louis Savary, Sound Health - The Music and Sound that Makes Us Whole

The Book of Sound Therapy by Olivia Dewhurst-Maddock, 1993.

Son of the Sun: The Life and Philosophy of Akhnaton, King of Egypt by Savitri Devi, 1946.

Hara: the Vital Center of Man by Karlfried Graf Durckheim, 2004.

The Fifth Agreement by Don Miguel Ruiz and Don Jose Ruiz, 2010.

Advanced Pranic Healing by Master Choa Kok Sui, 1992.

Emerald Tablets of Thoth the Atlantean by Doreal, 1996.

Living in the Heart by Drunvalo Melchizedek, 2003.

Shiva Sutras by Swami Lakshmanjoo, 2007. Self Realization in Kashmir Shaivism by Lakshmanjoo, 1994.

Power of Now by Eckhart Tolle, 1999.

Cancer: The Problem and the Solution by Dr. Johanna Budwig and Lothar Hirneise, 2008.

The Magnesium Miracle by Dr. Carolyn Dean, MD, ND (second edition, 2017)

HATHOR'S TEMPLE, DENDERA, EGYPT

THOTH and HATHOR

Thoth (god of wisdom) and Hathor (goddess of love, music and dance) are depicted as primal deities in ancient Egypt

138

With thanks and acknowledgements to the following authors who have contributed greatly with their inspiring articles toward the research of this book

Dr. Nelie Johnson, MD is a family physician and facilitator for healing - inspiring and guiding people to tap into their own healing potential. She is a contributing author to a bestselling book and provides seminars, workshops, and private consultations. *www.awarenessheals.ca*

Dr. Candace Pert, PhD is an internationally recognized pharmacologist who has published over 300 scientific articles on peptides and their receptors and the role of these neuropeptides in the immune system. Her earliest work as a researcher involved the discovery of opiate receptors and the actions of receptors. She has an international reputation in the field of receptor pharmacology and chemical neuroanatomy. Dr. Pert has lectured worldwide on these and other subjects, including her theories on emotions and mind-body communication. Her popular book, *"Molecules of Emotion, Why You Feel the Way You Feel,"* (Scribner, September 1997) expounds on her research and theories. She was featured in "Washingtonian" magazine (Dec. 2001) as one of Washington's fifty "Best and Brightest" individuals. *www.candacepert.com*

Tom Kenyon's life studies and many lifetimes of remembrances, complete with background knowledge and experience allow him to move with equal facility between Tibetan Buddhism, Egyptian High Alchemy, Taoism and Hinduism and the sciences relative to each. A workshop or teaching experience with him leaves you empowered with a vast body of knowledge suffused with tones that awaken all the physical centers, thus allowing for greater understanding of the words and Spirit imparted. *www.tomkenyon.com* and Virginia Essene's *sharefoundationnetwork.com*

Paul Hubbert and Ricardo B Serrano

Paul Hubbert, my Holograhic Sound Healing facilitator, August 2001, N. Vancouver. *www.holographicsound.com*

Alton Kamadon, my late Merkaba facilitator, and *Drunvalo Melchizedek*, the *Flower of Life* originator and author of *Living in the Heart, Serpent of Light* www.drunvalo.net

Dr Johanna Budwig's Diet for Cancer and Chronic Diseases, Udo Erasmus Fats that Heal Fats that Kill, Hira Ratan Manek's Sun Gazing, and *Dr. Richard Gerber*, author of *Vibrational Medicine: New Choices for Healing Ourselves*

Ricardo B Serrano, R.Ac.

Ricardo B. Serrano, R.Ac., a registered acupuncturist, author of Meditation and Qigong Mastery book with Omkabah Heart Lightbody Activation, Serpent of Light Omkabah, and Maitreya (Shiva) Shen Gong Procedure videos and other related meditation and healing books, Qi-healer and certified Qigong teacher/ founder of Maitreya (Shiva) Shen Gong and integrative Enlightenment Qigong. He has been trained by Pan Gu Shengong Master Ou Wen Wei, Wuji Qigong Master Michael Winn, Sheng Zhen Qigong Master Li Jun Feng, Master Pranic Healer Choa Kok Sui, Zhan Zhuang Qigong Master Richard Mooney, Merkaba Master Alton Kamadon, Qi Dao Master Lama Somananda Tantrapa, Toltec Master don Miguel Ruiz, Sri Vidya teacher Raja Choudhury and his other meditation, Qigong, herbal, nutrition and acupuncture teachers.

He has been practicing herbology, Qi-healing (Qigong with acupuncture) for over 30 years. He specializes in stress and pain management, cancer and chronic diseases, and alcohol and drug rehabilitation through natural healing alternative modalities such as counselling, meditation, nutrition, exercise, holographic sound healing, Qigong, Qi-healing, intranasal light therapy, EFT, acupuncture, herbology, acupressure.

He continues to educate his clients and everyone worldwide through his meditation and Qigong workshops, videos, and holistic websites at holisticwebs.com, innerway.ca, keystohealing.ca, qiwithoutborders.org, qigonghealer.com, freedomhealthrecovery.com, qigongmastery.ca, acutcmdetox.com. His books are: *Meditation and Qigong Mastery*, *Return to Oneness with the Tao, Return to Oneness with Spirit through Pan Gu Shen Gong, Return to Oneness with Shiva, Oneness with Shiva* and *The Cure & Cause of Cancer.*

The reality of this whole universe is God consciousness. It is filled with God consciousness.

This world is nothing but the blissful energy of the all-pervading consciousness of God. God and the individual are one, to realize this is the essence and goal of meditation and Qigong.

Whatever the diagnosis of your disease, you do not have to expect the worst. For every problem, there are solutions. You hold the keys to healing.

Made in the USA
Las Vegas, NV
14 November 2024

11814363R00079